Start To Navigate

Start to Navigate

Conrad Dixon

Adlard Coles Limited

Granada Publishing Limited
First published in Great Britain 1977
by Adlard Coles Limited
Frogmore St Albans Hertfordshire AL2 2NF and
Upper James Street London W1R 4BP

ISBN 229 11573 X

Printed in Great Britain by
Richard Clay (The Chaucer Press) Ltd
Bungay, Suffolk

Contents

– position by depth contour line – position from a line of soundings – a final exercise

Introduction

This book has two aims: to give the young crewman an understanding of what is going on in the cockpit and at the chart table, and to serve as an elementary textbook for fairly experienced yachtsmen studying for the RYA National Coastal or Yachtmaster certificates. The layout is such that the reader may make a natural progression from taking a foredeck interest in buoys, tides and courses to where he becomes competent to navigate an offshore yacht in strange waters. An old chart, parallel ruler, pair of dividers or compasses, a pencil and a soft rubber are all the tools needed in the early stages; a current copy of *Reed's Nautical Almanac* and a circular protractor are desirable optional extras.

Conrad Dixon
University of Exeter
1977

Chapter One

Buoys, marks and lights

The first ten minutes after getting away from the quayside, pontoon or mooring are a bustle of activity with fenders to be stowed, warps coiled and sails trimmed, but the time comes when all is shipshape above and below and, helmsman apart, the hands have time to look about them. Open water appears ahead and the first navigation buoys come bobbing and dipping into view. Logically, some will be left on one hand and some on the other, but which is which? This is the time to begin to learn the language of buoys and marks, which tells you all about the safe and dangerous areas of the sea and has a vocabulary based on shape, colour and topmark. Understand this code and you will be well on the way to grasping the whole art of pilotage in small craft.

The shape of buoys and beacons

Buoys have the four basic shapes shown in figure 1 and are conical – like an archbishop's mitre; can – resembling a tin of beans; spherical – as with a Christmas pudding; or pillar – looking very much like the above-water part of a fisherman's float. Buoys are moored floating marks that indicate the sides of navigable channels, show where danger lies, give the deepest water, or mark off special areas of the sea. For reasons of economy, or convenience, some floating marks are in spar form (figure 2) and look like sticks poking up out of the water. Figure 2 also gives the silhouettes of a beacon, a beacon tower and a withy. Beacons of wood, iron or steel are erected on shore or in shallow water to guide the mariner in the same way as buoys; beacon towers of stone or concrete are built on rocks to make them more easily seen; and withies – which are generally trunks or branches of trees with the butt end planted in sand or mud

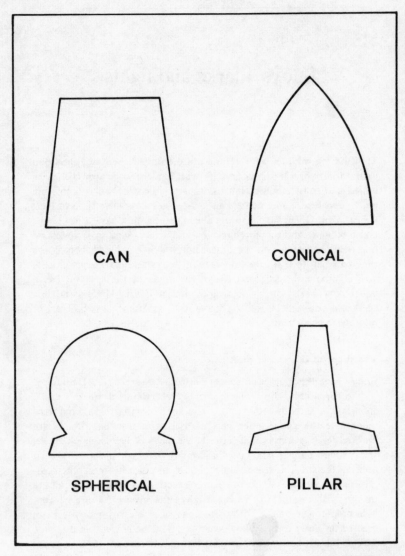

Fig. 1

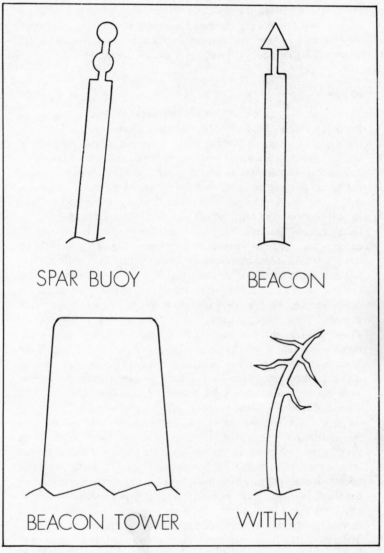

SPAR BUOY   BEACON

BEACON TOWER   WITHY

Fig. 2

– indicate shoal water in creeks and rivers. Shape gives the primary
clue to the meanings of buoys, and we must now go on to look at the
three systems of buoyage to be encountered in the waters of north-
west Europe, and see how shape, colour and topmark combine to tell
us on which side a buoy or fixed mark is to be passed.

System 'A'

This system began coming into effect in 1977, and combines all
the best features of the older lateral and cardinal systems. There are
five types of marks in System 'A'. *Lateral* marks give the form of
well-defined channels, while *cardinal* marks give the deepest water by
reference to a compass direction from a danger. *Isolated danger*
marks are perched on or moored over dangers of limited size, while
safe water marks show navigable water and are, for instance, found
in mid-channel. The fifth category of special marks relates to such
things as spoil grounds where your household refuse is disposed of,
and is of secondary importance to a navigator. Figure 3 may make all
this clearer, and some questions are written in to start you thinking.

Look at figure 3 and imagine that you have sailed away from
familiar waters and are entering Port Hero, a few miles down the
coast. The first buoy you see in the offing is an isolated danger buoy
marking Black Rock, a small, but dangerous, rock in the path of
shipping. What shape is it? (*Answer on page 117.*) The letters BRB
beneath the buoy symbol indicate that it is painted black with a red
horizontal band, and it has two black spheres as a topmark. It is an
isolated danger mark, and all you have to do is to pass it on either
side, but keeping a respectable distance off. Two buoys come into
view at the mouth of the harbour. What shapes are they? (*Answers
on page 117.*) The red one to port (on your left hand as you look
forward) has a topmark of the same shape and colour as the buoy
itself, while the green one to starboard (on your right hand as you
look forward) has a single green cone as topmark. Both buoys are
lateral (or side) marks giving the safe extent of a channel between two
headlands, and you enter harbour by going between them. Addition-
ally, Low Head has a fixed beacon on it with a cone topmark, and
that is a further indication of the starboard side of the entrance.
The rule is that when approaching from seaward, *red* can or spar
buoys with their optional *single* red can-shaped topmarks remain to
port – to the left; *green* conical or spar buoys with optional *single*

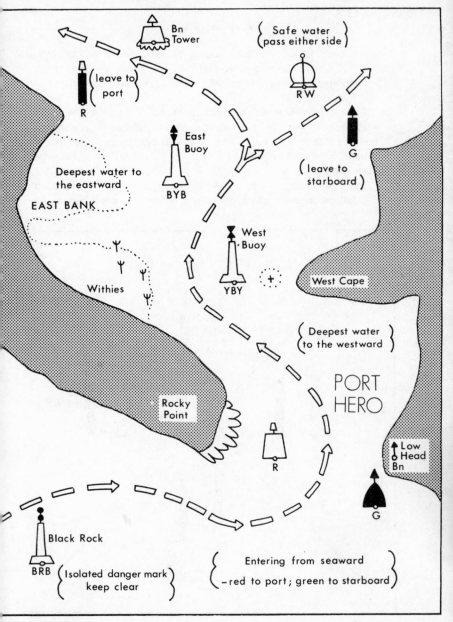

Fig. 3

green cone-shaped topmarks remain to starboard – to the right. Naturally, when leaving Port Hero and proceeding seawards the reverse applies with starboard marks left to port and port marks to starboard.

Your craft is now within the entrance, and West Cape lies ahead with the next buoy on the port bow. What is the shape of the next buoy? (*Answer on page 117.*) It has a *double* topmark and is painted black and yellow, the colours of a cardinal mark. Here we must digress for a moment to look at figure 4 which outlines the function of cardinal marks – to warn of danger in a certain direction and tell the mariner where the deepest water lies, and which is the

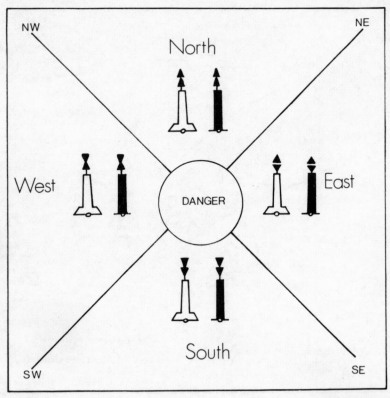

Fig. 4

safe side to pass, by reference to a compass direction. In figure 4 the north cardinal mark has a topmark of two upward-pointing black cones, meaning that the danger lies south of the buoy and the safe side to pass is the *northern* side. The cones of the south cardinal mark are downward-pointing, indicating that it should be passed on the *southern* side. Easterly cardinal marks have a topmark of two cones base to base to make a split diamond-shaped image, and are left to the westward as you pass to the *eastward*. Back to figure 3. West Buoy has an hourglass-shaped topmark of two cones point to point, and the significance is that shoal water lies to the east, so the *west* is the safe side to pass. East Buoy comes next. What shape is it? Which is the dangerous side? Which side should you pass? (*Answers on page 117*.) The spherical buoy with red and white vertical stripes and a *single* red sphere topmark is a safe water mark and has navigable water all round it, and the channel to the westward passes between a mark and a beacon tower. Describe the mark. (*Answer on page 117*.)

Special marks, denoting the existence of traffic separation lanes, spoil grounds, military exercise areas, cables, pipelines or recreation zones, are painted *yellow* and have *single* X-shaped topmarks, and the same markings are used for buoys fitted with meters for measuring tides and currents. New dangers, such as wrecks, and established ones in the form of middle ground shoals, are no longer specially buoyed but are treated like any other danger, a rock, for example, and marked with the lateral or cardinal marks according to their situation. Every system has its exceptions, but with System 'A' they are few. Occasionally, black may be substituted for green on starboard hand marks, while lightships and navigation buoys of the high focal plane type (very tall pillar buoys) are individually marked because of their special character. System 'A' is being introduced in the English Channel, North Sea and Baltic in the first instance, but some years will pass before all the coasts of north-west Europe are covered by it, and for that reason you have to know about the lateral and cardinal systems it replaces.

Lateral system

The basis of the lateral system is that buoyage is related to the general direction taken by the mariner when approaching from seaward, or the direction of the main stream of the flood tide, and figure 5

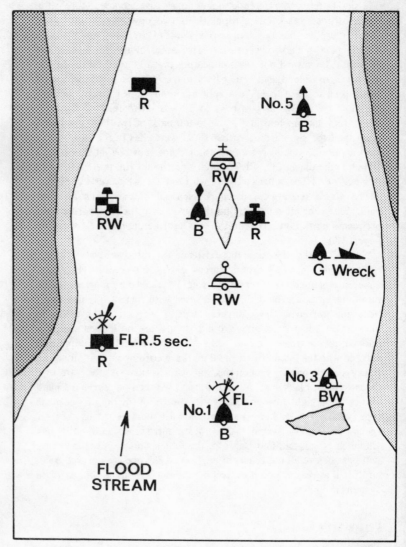

Fig. 5

illustrates its working. The flood tide runs northerly into a river mouth and, as in System 'A', the vessel coming in from seaward leaves the can-shaped buoys to port and the conical ones to starboard. The colours in the lateral system are black, or black and white chequers, or black and yellow chequers for the starboard hand buoys, and red, or red and white chequers, or red and yellow chequers for the port hand buoys. The topmarks are as in figure 6. In the middle of the river in figure 5, at each end of a shoal, are spherical middle ground buoys, and where the outer buoy is painted with horizontal

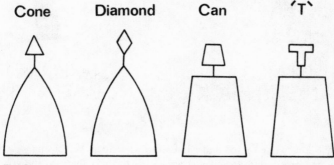

Fig. 6

red and white bands the meaning is that the main channel lies to starboard, or the channels are of equal importance, while black and white bands mean that the main channel is to port. The topmarks of middle ground buoys give additional information as to the side to pass, as outlined in the following table:

Main channel to Starboard	Channels of equal importance	Main channel to Port
Outer end – red can	Outer end – red sphere	Outer end – black cone
Inner end – red 'T'	Inner end – red cross	Inner end – black diamond

Spar buoys may be used as alternative marks in the lateral system: figure 7 shows, on the left, a red, white and black isolated danger spar buoy employed in place of the more usual spherical buoy in the same colours, while on the right is a starboard hand spar buoy, painted black and white and having a 'broom' topmark that looks like a cone from a distance. Pillar buoys are often used to mark the fairway, mid-channel or a landfall, and when so used are painted in

SPAR BUOYS

ISOLATED
DANGER MARK

STARBOARD
HAND MARK

Fig. 7

black and white or red and white vertical stripes. Wreck marks are
painted green, and are obeyed according to their shape in the same
way as port, starboard or middle ground marks.

Thus, in figure 5, the central buoy on the right hand side is a
green conical buoy without a topmark, and when travelling with the
flood stream you would leave it to starboard and thus keep clear of
the dangerous wreck between the buoy and the shore. When spar
buoys are used to mark wrecks, the lower part is painted red or black
to indicate whether it is a port or starboard hander: middle ground
wreck buoys are spherical, and can be left on either hand. Other
buoys are more garishly coloured. Yellow is for a quarantine
anchorage; yellow and black for outfall and spoil ground buoys
that mark the seaward ends of sewer pipes, and sludge and rubbish
dumping grounds respectively. Buoys showing the limits of military
exercise areas are either red and yellow and marked DZ for Danger
Zone, or blue and white and marked DA for Danger Area. Pillar
buoys with red and yellow vertical stripes in fluorescent paint are
Ocean Data Acquisition System (ODAS) buoys moored for research
purposes, while spherical buoys marked CABLE are guarding the
inshore ends of telegraph cables and warning you against anchoring

in their vicinity. The Lateral System has been in general use in British waters for some time, and the changeover to System 'A' will not be completed until the 1980s.

Cardinal System

Figure 8 outlines the main feature of the cardinal system of buoyage – the use of topmarks to give the direction of dangers. The north and south marks may be single or double cones: the east and west marks are the same as in System 'A'. The shape and colour of a mark will tell you what it means in cases where a topmark is not fitted, as the following table shows:

	North Quadrant	South Quadrant	East Quadrant	West Quadrant
Buoy Shape	Conical or spar	Can or spar	Conical, spar or ogival	Can, spindle or spar
Colour	Black with a white stripe	Red with a white band	Red over white	Black over white
Meaning	Pass to the northward	Pass to the southward	Pass to the eastward	Pass to the westward

Two new terms appear here: an ogival buoy is a slimmed-down conical buoy; a spindle buoy looks like a fatter, tapered spar buoy. Another feature of the system is that wreck marks are placed only in the east and west quadrants; they are identical in shape to navigational marks, but are coloured green. The cardinal system is superior on a rocky coast with many detached dangers, but cannot compare to the lateral system for marking intricate channels among sandbanks and shoals. Where the two systems meet, transition marks are to be found – these generally take the form of buoys painted *diagonally* with red and white or black and white stripes.

Some words of caution

The most important thing about buoys is not to get too close to them. They are fairly unyielding if the tide happens to carry your vessel onto one of them, and as they sometimes ground on the very banks or dangers they are supposed to mark, a wide berth is a good rule to observe. Buoys are taken away for a repaint at intervals, and sometimes drift away from their charted positions, so that they cannot be relied on for navigational purposes. They are advisory marks, and not in the same class as fixed beacons whose position is accurately charted.

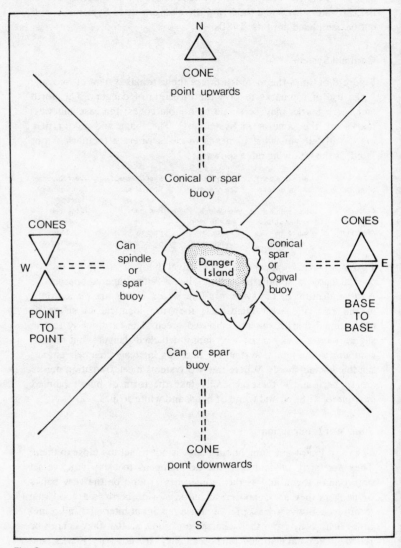

Fig. 8

In figure 9, the position of all three beacons is the central dot; the one on the left is a plain beacon, the central one is painted red and white and the right hand beacon is green and has a green cone topmark. What is the significance of the third beacon to a mariner approaching a harbour from seaward? (*Answer on page 117.*) The probable position of a buoy marked on a chart is the small circle at its base, but as it swings about on its mooring chain under the influence of wind, tide or current the actual position may be

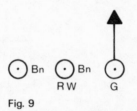

Fig. 9

anywhere within the radius of that mooring chain. Beacon towers do not always follow buoyage rules closely, and while they are generally painted red, or partially red, when acting as port hand marks, and black or green with added bands of white when acting as starboard hand markers, you must be prepared to find white, grey and pink towers, or even some painted red and black.

Radar reflectors fitted to many buoys are metal plates slotted or welded together to provide right-angled surfaces to reflect radar transmissions, and are sometimes confused with diamond-shaped topmarks. Where topmark and radar reflector are both fitted to a buoy there need be no confusion; the topmark is, as the name suggests, on top. Curiously enough, although in real life the topmark is fitted above the radar reflector, on older charts the topmark is shown attached to the buoy with the five-fingered symbol of a radar reflector suspended above it. The shape of buoys is given on charts, and the only representation that seems to cause difficulty is that of the pillar buoy, or its taller relatives the high focal plane and lighthouse buoys. Figure 10a depicts the obsolescent symbol: figure 10b, the up-to-date representation of the type. What is the function of the buoy at 10a? (*Answer on page 117.*) It is a lighted buoy showing an interrupted quick flashing light – a number of quick flashes followed by a long eclipse – and is fitted with a radar reflector. What is the function of the buoy shown in 10b? (*Answer on page 117*.) At night, the shape, topmark and colouring of a buoy are hard to make out, except in bright moonlight and at close range, and identification is generally

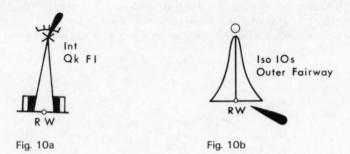

Fig. 10a   Fig. 10b

made by reference to two factors – the rhythm of a light and its colour.

Fixed lights

Fixed lights have no rhythm – they are exhibited without interruption or change of characteristics. A fixed light may mark the end of a jetty, a beacon or be fitted to a buoy, and the prefix F at the beginning of the description of the light on the chart, or in one of the volumes of the *Admiralty List of Lights and Fog Signals*, signifies that it is a fixed light. Thus, the legend '2 F W (vert)' describes two fixed white lights, disposed vertically, such as those which mark the end of Skegness Pier, while 'F Vi' denotes a fixed violet light, as fitted to the end of the jetty at Roscoff. In navigable rivers, such as the Thames, the chart will show a large number of wharves on both sides of the river marked '2 F R (vert)', indicating that these projections into navigable water carry two red vertical lights to warn shipping that they are there. As the rationalization of buoyage proceeds, those obstructions on the *starboard* side of waterways, as one approaches from seaward, will be marked by single or double *green* fixed lights, with red lights reserved for the port side of the channel.

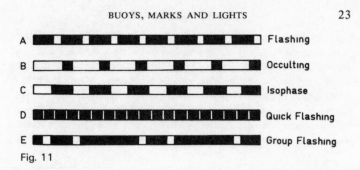

A   Flashing
B   Occulting
C   Isophase
D   Quick Flashing
E   Group Flashing

Fig. 11

Rhythmic, or flashing, lights

The appearance of the five main types of rhythmic lights is given in figure 11. A flashing light is more dark than light, and has a regular rhythm, while an occulting light is more light than dark and looks a little like a lizard blinking. Isophase lights have equal periods of light and darkness, and the notation 'Iso 4 sec.' means that two seconds of steady white light are followed by two seconds of darkness, and so on. A quick flashing light winks away at 50–60 flashes a minute, while a very quick flashing (VQk Fl) light gives 100–120 flashes a minute. Group flashing is where two or more flashes are repeated at regular intervals, and group occulting is a similar pattern with periods of darkness grouped by number. A long flash is one of over two seconds' duration, and Morse Code flashes (look for 'Mo' in the light description) are the appropriate letters of the code. Finally, there are alternating lights that show a change of colour on the same bearing, and are often found on fixed marks.

Identification of lights

Buoyage systems are subject to frequent revision, and although these changes are notified in the weekly editions of *Admiralty Notices to Mariners* it may be some time before knowledge of them reaches the small craft owner and user. Consequently, you should be aware of the general principles behind the light code of the system in operation, and the table on page 25 may be helpful.

Identification of buoys

The identification of buoys should be systematic rather than haphazard, and it will be instructive to pick out the buoys on your old chart and then look at *Admiralty Chart 5011* to see exactly what their function is. *Chart 5011*, which is not a chart at all but a booklet, gives the meanings of symbols and abbreviations used on Admiralty charts, and you should be able with its assistance, or with the help of the diagrams in the first few pages of *Reed's Nautical Almanac*, to identify buoys quite readily. There are six questions you have to ask yourself every time you want to identify a buoy, and the Six-Question Method becomes automatic with a little practice. Figure 12 gives the outline

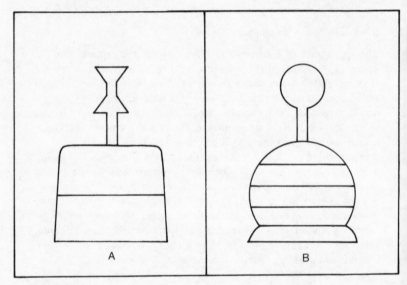

Fig. 12

of two navigation buoys: fill in the details as you puzzle out the answers, and then turn to page 117 to see how you have fared.

	Buoy 'A'	Buoy 'B'
Shape?		
Topmark?		
Which system?		
Colour of buoy?		
Function?		
Meaning?		

LIGHT CODES FOR BUOYAGE AND NAVIGATION MARK SYSTEMS

MARK	LATERAL	SYSTEM 'A'	CARDINAL
Port	Red: 1–4 Fl White: even no.	Red: any	White: odd no.
Starboard	White: odd no.	Green: any	Red/White: odd no.
Cardinal (N)		White: Qk Fl/V Qk Fl	Red/White: even no.
Cardinal (E)		White: Qk Fl or V Qk Fl (3)	
Cardinal (S)		White: Qk Fl or V Qk Fl (6) and long flash.	
Cardinal (W)		White: Qk Fl of V Qk Fl (9) and long flash.	White: even no.
Iso. Danger	Rhythmic	White: Gp Fl (2)	Rhythmic
Safe Water	Rhythmic	White: Iso, Occ, Fl	Rhythmic
Special		Yellow: distinctive	
Wreck (port)	Green: Fl (2)		Green: Fl (West)
Wreck (starboard)	Green: Fl (3)		Green: Int. Fl (East)
Wreck (middle)	Green: Occ; Int. Qk Fl		
Wreck Vessel	Green: fixed		
ODAS	Blue/White: Int. Qk Fl	Blue/White: Int. Qk Fl	

Chapter Two

Charts

Now that you have become familiar with the navigational symbols on charts we can go ahead with the use of them. Charts are underwater contour maps with added information on what may be seen on the surface and, because they are flat representations of parts of the curved surface of the earth, a certain amount of juggling has gone on to get them ready for use at sea.

In 1569 a learned Lowlander called Gerardus Mercator got the idea of drawing all the pole-to-pole meridians parallel to each other so that lines drawn on the chart cut these meridians at the same angle and enabled the laying off of long course lines for ships to follow. The inevitable distortion arising from use of this method was compensated for by putting the parallels of latitude further and further apart as the chart depicted areas more distant from the equator. The most important consequence for our purposes is that when using a Mercator projection we have to be careful how we measure distances from charts, and now you should keep an eye on figure 13 as the explanation proceeds.

Distances

Charts have scales at top and bottom and at each side, but when measuring distance we totally ignore the top and bottom scales, and concentrate on the side ones. Figure 13 shows the top left-hand corner of a chart, and in the bottom left-hand corner is marked the position of a yacht at 1315 hours by 24-hour notation. The equivalent civil time would be 1.15 pm, but the navigator uses 24-hour notation exclusively. The 'fixed' position is the dot within the circle, and 1315 is the time it was at that fixed position. In figure 13 the yacht is shown moving away to another fixed position at 1330 hours, and then heading away northward.

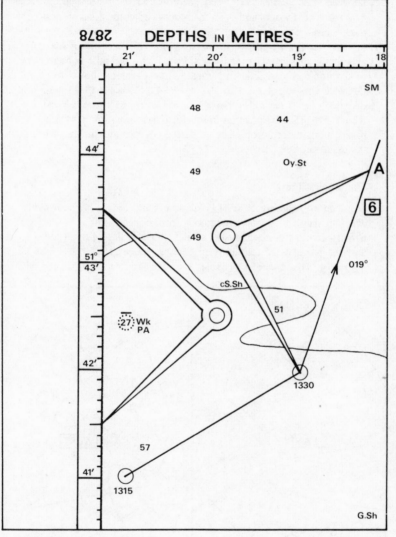

Fig. 13

Imagine that you want to find out how far the yacht has travelled between leaving the 1330 fixed position and the point marked 'A'. You take the dividers and open them out to span the distance between these points and then carry them across to the side scale roughly opposite to the length we are measuring. This scale is in sea miles and tenths of sea miles (called 'cables'), and a sea mile is equivalent to a minute of latitude. In figure 13 the dividers shown touching the scale markings measure from 51° 41·5′ N to 51° 43·5′ N – a distance of two sea miles. Now it is your turn. Measure the distance from the 1315 fixed position to the 1330 fixed position, remembering to use the side scale opposite to where you are measuring. What is the distance? (*Answer on page 117.*)

Gnomonic Charts

Some charts, notably those of Polar waters and certain harbour plans, are constructed on the Gnomonic (pronounced with a silent 'g') principle with the meridians as straight lines radiating from the pole and the parallels of latitude representing concentric circles – as in figure 14. This treatment enables the mariner to obtain great circle

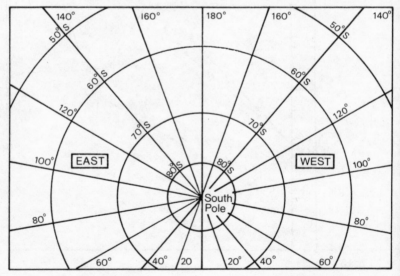

Fig. 14

tracks — a great circle is one whose plane passes through the centre of the earth and its surface path represents the shortest distance between two points on the earth — but they then have to be transferred to a Mercator chart to work out the courses to steer. From our point of view it does not matter that the information under the title of the chart includes the fact that it is based on either the Mercator or Gnomonic projection, for we use both types indiscriminately as if they were flat and literal representations of land and sea. If you would be happier knowing the precise difference between the two projections at this stage I suggest you leaf forward to page 70 and contrast figure 33 with figure 14 to set your mind at rest.

Speed

Speed is measured in knots, and a knot is a navigational unit of speed of one sea mile an hour. A sea mile is 1,852 metres, 6,076·12 feet or 2,025·37 yards long — about 15 per cent longer than a land mile. In sea navigation there are two sorts of speed — speed through the water and speed over the ground. Speed through the water is fairly self-evident; speed over the ground is sometimes also called effective speed, ground speed or speed made good, but they all mean real progress across the chart, whereas speed through the water is what the boat is trying to do before wind, current or tide speed it up or slow it down, or push it to one side or the other. Speed through the water is measured by a towed log, an impeller-driven log fitted in the hull which records on a car-type speedometer, or by pressure recorders, but until doppler speedometers (which can measure distance travelled over the seabed in shallow water by comparing echo frequencies) become common, speed over the ground will continue to need calculation.

In figure 13 we knew by measurement that the yacht had made good two sea miles between the 1330 fix and position 'A': if the time taken was twenty minutes, we can work out that in taking one-third of an hour to cover two sea miles the speed over the ground was six sea miles an hour, or six knots. What the log shows is second-best information which may correspond with what we have found out, but which equally well may not. Speed measured by the log is, as we shall see later, useful when working out dead (deduced) reckoning, which is based solely on course and speed through the water,

and these distinctions will be given further emphasis in Chapters
Seven and Eight when we start plotting in real earnest.

Depths

The Hydrographic Department has been going quietly metric since
1968, and new charts give depths in metres from 21 metres onwards
and in metres and decimetres (tenths of a metre) for depths below 21
metres. Where the data is sufficiently precise, depths between 21 and
31 metres may be expressed in half-metres. Depths are also called
soundings, and *Chart 5011* gives the full range of symbols used.
Some common examples appear below:

(1)	(2)	(3)	(4)
$\overset{\cdot}{\underline{180}}$	59	12_5	$\underline{0_9}$
Meaning:	*Meaning:*	*Meaning:*	*Meaning:*
No bottom found at 180 metres	A depth of water of 59 metres	A depth of water of 12 metres, 5 decimetres	Dries 90 centimetres (9 decimetres)

Older charts have the information in fathoms and feet (a fathom is
six feet), and the roughly equivalent chart markings would be:

(1)	(2)	(3)	(4)
$\overset{\cdot}{\underline{100}}$	32	6_5	$\underline{3}$
Meaning:	*Meaning:*	*Meaning:*	*Meaning:*
No bottom found at 100 fathoms	A depth of water of 32 fathoms	A depth of water of 6 fathoms, 5 feet	Dries 3 feet

Metric charts show land coloured by a flat buff tint, drying areas in
green, and blue for water of less than five metres in depth. Magenta
is used to call attention to lighted buoys, separation zones, anchorages
and dumping grounds.

Charts not only give the depth of water but also convey information about the nature of the bottom, and in figure 13 you can see
some examples. SM means sand and mud, cS Sh is coarse sand and
shells, while Oy St stands for oyster shells and stones. Page S of
Chart 5011 lists the abbreviations in current use and, after looking
through the list, it would be good practice to name the following for

yourself. (a) sy Cy, (b) so Oz, (c) f G, (d) Wd. (*Answers on page 117*.) The nature of the bottom as shown by the chart can help to give a boats position, and it is also important to know what obstructions exist on the sea bed and what is the depth of water over them. The waters around the British Isles abound in wrecks and you should know which are harmless to your craft, and which are not.

Wrecks

Look at figure 15: we will start with the old and innocent, and end with the new and downright dangerous. The first symbol indicates a wreck over which the exact depth of water is unknown but is thought to be more than 28 metres, and its position is only approximately known. Symbol 2 is in the same category, but its position is known. Symbol 3 denotes a wreck where the site has been swept by a wire drag to the depth shown so that there is at least a clearance of 32 metres, while wreck number 4 has had the depth of water over it established by sounding. Symbol 5 is unsurveyed, but is considered to have a safe clearance of 27 metres, while 6, also unsurveyed, has less than 28 metres clearance and in big-ship terms is considered a danger to surface navigation. Symbols 7 and 8 stand for visible or partly-visible wrecks, and number 7 will almost certainly be marked by a buoy or buoys. These last two are a danger to even the smallest craft, and it is distinctly unwise to navigate in their vicinity.

System 'A' ends the distinctive marking of wrecks, and an appreciation of the meanings of the eight types of chart symbols denoting the existence of a wreck will help you determine the reason for the presence of a cardinal mark in an unexpected place.

More about charts

On picking up an Admiralty chart always look first of all at the bottom margin to find the date of publication. The usual formula goes something like this: 'Published at Taunton 30th May 1976 under the Superintendence of Rear-Admiral G. P. D. Hall, CB, DSC, Hydrographer of the Navy'. The more recent the publication date the more likely the chart is correct, but this is not the only yardstick of value to employ, for some charts with quite ancient publication dates will nevertheless have been updated and be wholly correct. The next place to look is the bottom right-hand corner where a phrase such as

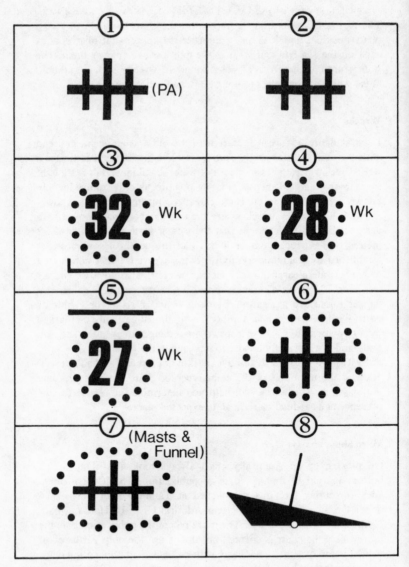

Fig. 15

'New Edition 3rd July, 1976' will indicate that a complete revision has taken place and the chart is up-to-date. The title block will give the scale of the chart, for example 1:25,000, and tell you that depths are in metres and heights on land in metres above Mean High Water Springs. The external thumblabel carries the title of the chart, its number and date of printing, and there is space to insert your own reference number and folio letter so that when the chart is stowed in a drawer it can be drawn out for use without disturbing its neighbours. Corrections to charts should be made from *Notices to Mariners* (a weekly publication) with waterproof violet ink, and a typical correction would read something like this:

1. 'A black spar buoy is to be inserted in position 177° 3,850 feet from Platte Fougère light (49° 30′ 50″ N 2° 29′ 10″ w approx.).
2. The small circle, Bn., (letters PC), close NW of the buoy in 1. is to be expunged. (On chart 3400 it is to be replaced by a small rock.)'

This means that you put a stroke through the beacon, measure and plot the position for the new spar buoy (as will be described in Chapter Five), and draw in the symbol, not forgetting to add the letter 'B' underneath it to show its colour. When replacing one symbol with another do not try to superimpose the new on the old; it is far better to delete the obsolete symbol neatly, draw in the new one nearby and link them by arrow. When you have made a permanent correction of this kind you should make a note of it by adding its *Notices to Mariners* number to the list for the current year in the bottom left margin of the chart where the words 'Small Corrections' are printed. Temporary or preliminary corrections are made in pencil, and where a major revision of a small part of a chart takes place you will have to paste on a printed block containing the new information supplied as part of *Notices to Mariners*.

Finally, do not omit to read the cautions and advice printed beneath or near the title block on the chart; they relate to items such as telegraph cables, shipping movements, submarine exercise areas, recommended channels, buoys not shown on the chart, traffic regulations and shifting sandbanks, and will stop you making a fool of yourself by running aground, going the wrong way, or anchoring in a forbidden place.

The Compass Rose

Charts embody one or more compass roses such as is illustrated in figure 16. They take the form of two concentric circles and are divided into 360°, with the outer ring marked every 10° and the inner ring every 30°. The outer circle expresses true direction relative to the geographical North and South Poles, and is used to set true

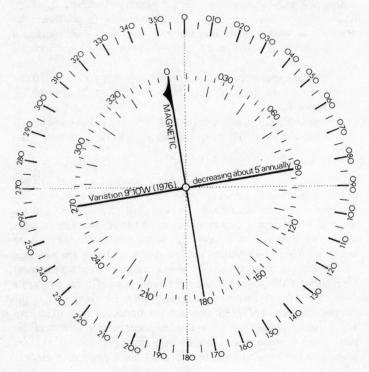

Fig. 16

courses or plot true bearings. The innner circle is oriented so that its North point is directly towards the Magnetic North Pole, and in figure 16 you will see the word *magnetic* printed alongside the North-South axis. Courses and bearings set from this inner circle are termed 'magnetic', and within the inner circle you can see additional marks representing the cardinal points – south-west, north north-east, etc. These cardinal markings come in handy when you want to give the helmsman an approximate course to steer while you are working out the correct course.

In figure 17 you must imagine a yacht just leaving port and making for the open sea. The navigator knows that the tide is favourable, his chart is modern and that there are no dangers ahead of him. He puts the parallel ruler on the chart with one edge representing the intended track the yacht will follow, carries it carefully across to the compass rose and notes that the ruler passes through the central dot and the marking for North East. A north-easterly course will see the yacht clear of the land, and the appropriate order is passed to the helmsman. On short passages in wooden or GRP yachts and using up-to-date charts this kind of coarse navigation is occasionally acceptable, but where the navigator has to contend with strong tides, leeway and compass deviation it will seldom give the best results.

Parallel rulers and plotters

The extending bar type of plastic parallel ruler was featured in figure 17, and the type has the twin advantages of cheapness and of being able to read chart detail through the transparent material. Its chief disadvantages are that it is inclined to slip at folds in the chart, or on damp patches, and that a downward pressure must be maintained on the static bar as the mobile bar is pushed forward. Roller rulers are heavier, and can be trundled easily over the chart on their little wheels, but are expensive and tend to take charge in a seaway unless secured – careering to and fro across the chart table until they acquire enough momentum to jump the fiddle and crash down on the cabin sole. Captain Field's parallel rules are variants of the extending bar and roller types with degrees incised on them. This means that they can double as protractors and, when lined up on a meridian, give an instant true course or bearing to the nearest 10°. This combination of protractor and ruler is a feature of most patent plotters, of which the two best known are the Hurst plotter and the Sestrel-Luard Navigator. With these instruments, a circular protractor, or rose, is aligned to either true or magnetic north, and the ruler arm swung round to get bearings and courses. Which type is best? I believe in simplicity and cheapness, and the plain, plastic,

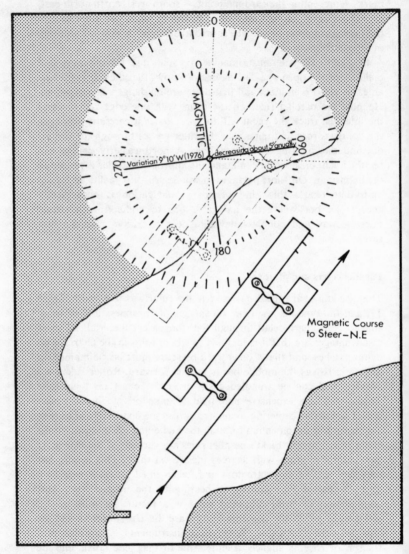

Fig. 17

extending bar type of parallel ruler proves most serviceable in the long run.

Now for some questions. In figure 17, use your parallel ruler to determine the true course to be followed by a vessel taking its departure from the south-eastern tip of the pier and making for the dot between 'N' and 'E'. Secondly, write down what you think would happen if a vessel took her departure from the pier and sailed on a true course of 010°? (*Answers on page 118.*)

Other charts and publications

Charts are expensive items nowadays, but fortunately the Hydrographer of the Navy prints and distributes instructional charts on thin paper which are ideal for practice purposes, and are cheap to buy. If you have not used one before, start with *Chart 5050*, which covers the coast from Falmouth to Plymouth, or get *Charts 5052* and *5053* of the English Channel. These are most useful for coastal work.

Not everybody uses Admiralty charts, and in small craft where space is at a premium the Stanford's series which fold up to 6 in × 10 in may prove ideal. Stanford's colours are blue for water, white for land and yellow-brown for drying areas; magnetic courses to steer, tidal chartlets and harbour plans are superimposed, and the backs contain useful local information. The magazine *Yachting Monthly* publishes local pilot books such as *East Coast Rivers* and *West Country Rivers* which are invaluable when exploring confined waters, while the *Cruising Association Handbook* has a wealth of detail about approaches and harbours. The admirable little Castrol booklet covers the principal yachting centres, and bulkier works like the *North Brittany Pilot* and *North Sea Harbours and Pilotage* published by Adlard Coles Limited are essential for voyaging cross-Channel. Last, but by no means least, comes *Reed's Nautical Almanac*. This hardy annual contains in potted form all you need to know about first aid and harbour signals, radiobeacons and collision regulations. The navigator should make it his 'best buy', for the tidal information and section on visual navigation aids give in compact form the basic data for successful and worry-free passages.

Chapter Three

Tides

One of the first facts we assimilate in childhood is that if we build a sandcastle too far down the beach the sea comes up and washes it away and, while the up-and-down movement of the tide is readily understood, it may not be quite so easy to appreciate that the surface of the sea is also moving horizontally. Tides move vertically and tidal streams horizontally, but there is a common explanation in that the pull of the Moon, and to a lesser extent the Sun, causes the water to pile up and drain away to give in northern Europe two high and two low tides every day.

Explanation of Tides

Look at figure 18. In (1) we assume that the earth wears a uniform mantle of water, while in (2) you must think of the earth revolving within its influenced ellipsoid of water so that, as a general rule, two high and two low tides are experienced every day. In (3) the ellipsoid is influenced by the Moon and Sun pulling in conjunction to give above-average high tides, and in (4) the Moon and Sun are in opposition and stretching the ellipsoid of water to its limits so as to give the highest, or Spring, tides. Neap tides are illustrated in (5) where the Sun and Moon operate at right angles and the range of tides is least. How powerful are the Sun and Moon respectively? It is generally accepted that the Sun has just under half the attractive force of the Moon. Now we must define some terms.

Definitions

The *range* of tide is the vertical distance in feet or metres between the level at any high tide and the preceding or following low tide. The

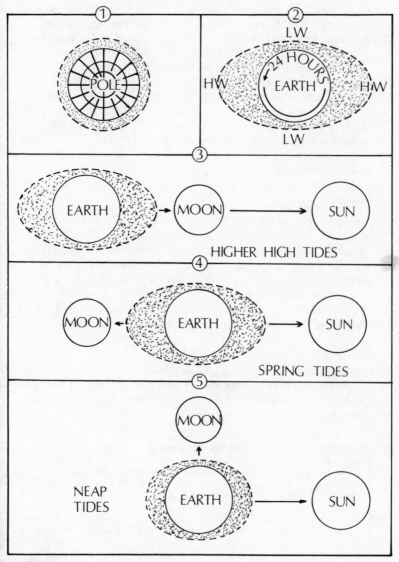

Fig. 18

rise of tide is the difference between high water and chart datum. *Chart datum* is the plane from which sea depths are measured to give *soundings*, and on modern charts it approximates to *Lowest Astronomical Tide* (*L.A.T.*), which is the lowest level of water you could reasonably expect to experience under average meteorological conditions and any combination of astronomical conditions. The *height* of tide is the vertical distance at any given moment between chart datum and water level, and the *depth* of water is the sum of the height of tide and the charted sounding. *Duration* is the time elapsing between successive high and low tides, and the *rate* of a tidal stream is its horizontal movement in terms of knots and tenths of knots (sea miles per hour).

Springs and neaps

Spring tides occur every fortnight or so about a day and a half after new moon and full moon, and neaps about halfway between successive spring tides. Figure 19 gives a visual explanation of the difference between springs and neaps; springs give the highest and lowest tides, while at neaps the tidal range is more modest. From the practical point of view this means that at springs the tidal streams are much stronger, but the danger of grounding is greater; at neaps you can take a few liberties in shoal water, but get less help from a favourable tide.

Tide tables

Tables have been compiled to give the predicted daily rise of the tide at various ports and, while the layout of these tables varies, the information they give is fairly constant. *Reed's Nautical Almanac* tables have it set out in six columns.

AUGUST		High Water at Falmouth			
All times are GMT. Add one hour March 21 to October 24 to get BST					
Day of month	Day of week	Time h. min	Ht. m	Time h. min	Ht. m
1	Tu	0907	4·6	2141	4·7
2	W	1003	4·8	2247	4·6
3	Th	1115	4·4	2357	4·2

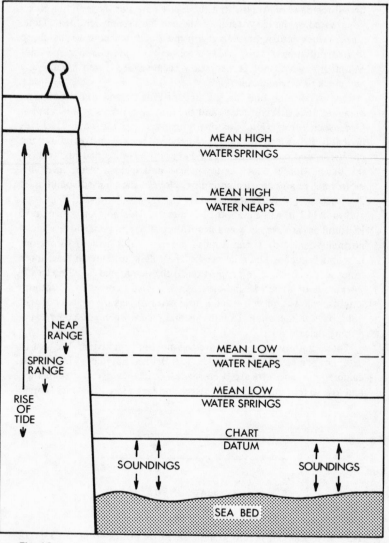

Fig. 19

The table gives the times of high water at Falmouth, Cornwall, for the first three days of August, but the figures are not those indicated by your watch or the clock on the bulkhead but Greenwich Mean Time, and for each four-figure entry you must add one hour to match up to British Summer Time. Of course, between late October and mid-March this would not be necessary because Greenwich Mean Time and clock time would coincide.

Let us take the line for the 2nd of August and run through its meaning. It is a Wednesday, and the first high tide is at 1103 BST – Greenwich Mean Time plus one hour. At 1103 the water level will probably (for these are only predictions) be 4·8 metres above the charted soundings in the port of Falmouth. The second high tide of the day is due at 2347 and you can anticipate a water level 4·6 metres above any charted sounding. Now, if the charted sounding is 3·2 metres, the depth of water at 1103 will be about 8 metres, and at 2347 it will be about 7·8 metres. This sort of information is useful in two ways; it enables a deep-draught vessel to use areas normally denied to it, and it helps the small craft owner to work out how much anchor chain he needs. The rule is to allow at least three times as much chain in proportion to the depth, and 8×3 metres is 24 metres or about 13 fathoms. Anchor chain comes in 15-fathom lengths, and as you will want a little extra to be sure the anchor will hold, pay out the whole 15 fathoms and secure when you come to the joining shackle.

The Admiralty tide tables are the most informative and easiest to use: no corrections are needed for British Summer Time – the calculations have already been made – and they give times of high and low water with heights in metres and feet. Here is a typical entry:

		MARCH	
	Time	m	ft
	0135	0·2	0·6
Th	0732	6·4	20·9
16	1341	0·4	1·3
	1933	6·5	21·2

Note that you can readily obtain the range of tide from this kind of table. For example, for the afternoon of Thursday 16th March at this particular port the range of tide is 6·5 minus 0·4 metres, making 6·1 metres. Further, they can help you to decide whether or not your vessel will remain afloat alongside a harbour wall at all states of the tide. Imagine that your draught is five feet and that the harbour plan shows 0₄ as the depth at your berthing point. During the night the depth of water at low tide is predicted as 0·6 plus 4 feet, making 4·6 feet, so you are likely to take the ground. On the afternoon low tide, however, with 1·3 feet plus 4 feet making 5·3 feet you will probably remain afloat. What do you think the depth of water would be at 0434 hours? (*Answers on page 118.*)

Secondary ports

It would be manifestly impossible to compile tide tables for every port, so many less important harbours are designated secondary ports and for tidal purposes are linked to a suitable standard port nearby by means of a calculated Tidal Difference.

Let us use the Falmouth data from page 40 as the basis for an example. It is Wednesday the 2nd of August and you are anchored off Newlyn, having previously arranged to go alongside briefly at morning high water to pick up stores. You look up the time of high water at the standard port — in this case Falmouth — and find it is 1003 GMT, or 1103 BST. *Reed's Nautical Almanac* reveals that the Tidal Difference for Newlyn in relation to Falmouth is minus twenty minutes, and 1103 minus 20 gives 1043 as the time of morning high water at Newlyn on the 2nd of August.

The Twelfth's Rule

So much for high and low water; now to obtain the height of tide or the depth of water at other times. For this purpose we use the Twelfth's Rule, and you should keep an eye on figure 20 as the explanation proceeds. The duration of a tide is just over six hours as a general rule, and most of the movement takes place in the middle two hours. We divide the predicted range of the tide into twelve parts and reckon that in the first hour the water will rise or fall by one-twelfth, in the second by two-twelfths and in the third by three-twelfths. In the fourth hour it will rise or fall another three-twelfths, in the fifth two-twelfths and in the sixth one-twelfth. In figure 20 the range of tide is a convenient 4·8 metres which facilitates a division into twelfths, but in real life things are seldom that easy. Try the

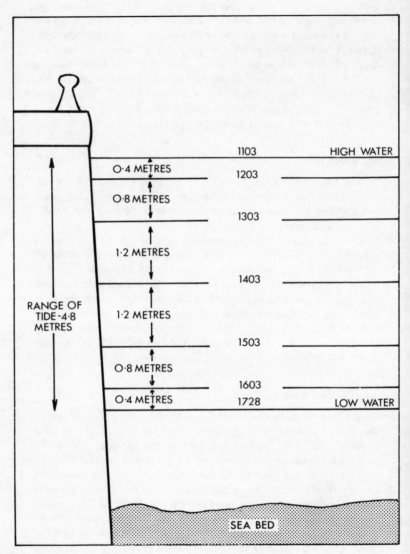

Fig. 20

following problems using the data from page 42 which, for convenience, are set out again below in abbreviated form.

	Time	m	ft
Th	0135	0·2	0·6
16	0732	6·4	20·9

Questions:

1. What would you expect the depth of water to be at 0235?
2. When will the height of tide be 3 metres?
3. If the charted sounding is one fathom, at about what time will you find 22 feet of water under your vessel?

(*Answers on page 118*).

Tidal stream diamonds

Information on the strength and direction of tidal streams comes from a number of sources: from *Admiralty Sailing Directions*, from *Reed's Nautical Almanac*, from the *Admiralty Tidal Stream Atlases*

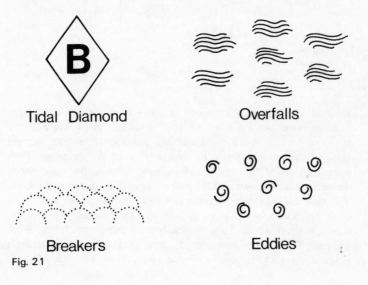

Tidal Diamond   Overfalls

Breakers   Eddies

Fig. 21

and from the tidal chartlets in *Reed's* or those printed on Stanford's charts. I will deal with the information on Admiralty charts first because it is often readily at hand on the chart you are using. Charts give details of areas to keep away from as well as conveying useful tidal stream information, and you should be able to recognise both types of symbols. In figure 21 appear the markings for overfalls, breakers and eddies – all to be avoided – and the tidal diamond symbol. The latter relates to the general area where it is printed, and a table relating to the diamond will be printed elsewhere on the chart and convey the information in tabular form, as follows:

		◇D	(position of diamond) Rate (knots)	
	Hours	Direction	Springs	Neaps
Before HW at	6	013°		
standard	5	023°	0·3 slack	0·1
	4	027°	0·8	0·4
port	3	023°	1·1	0·5
	2	023°	1·0	0·5
	1	017°	0·7	0·4
High Water		354°	0·5	0·2
	1	214°	0·7	0·3
	2	208°	0·9	0·4
	3	207°	1·1	0·5
After HW at	4	201°	1·2	0·6
standard	5	187°	0·6	0·3
port	6	120°	0·1	0·1

How do we use this information? In figure 22 at 1000 hours a yacht is at position 'A' close to the tidal diamond. High water at the standard port is at 12 noon and the almanac shows that we are between springs and neaps. By interpolation of the spring and neap figures given for two hours before high water in the table above we settle on a direction of 023° and a rate of three-quarters of a knot. You must imagine that the yacht is without motive power and that it drifts helplessly from 'A' to 'B' with the tidal stream, as is represented in figure 22 by the short line bearing three arrowheads. What we have done is to complete the first part of the tidal triangle – the effect of tidal stream for one hour. The intention of those

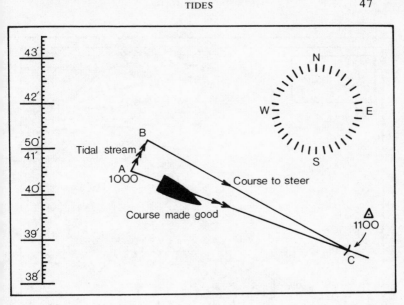

Fig. 22

on board is to voyage to 'C', and the navigator has drawn in the line 'A'–'C' to represent the track down which the yacht will travel, but it should be quite apparent that if he tried to steer down the track the tide would push the yacht away to port. The yacht can make 5·1 knots, and to get the true course to steer the navigator takes up a pair of compasses, sets them to 5·1 miles on the distance scale, puts the point on 'B' and cuts the track line near 'C'. He draws in 'B'–'C' and carries it across to the compass rose to get the true course to steer of 120°. The yacht will crab along 'A'–'C' with its bow to starboard to counteract the influence of the tide. The tidal diamond and table have given the necessary information to obtain the true course to steer.

Tidal stream atlases

These consist of thirteen chartlets giving predicted tidal streams at hourly intervals in relation to a major port, such as Dover. The strength of the tide is given emphasis by the heaviness of the arrows used to show direction, and the mean spring and neap rates are given alongside. In figure 23 a representation of part of a tidal atlas page

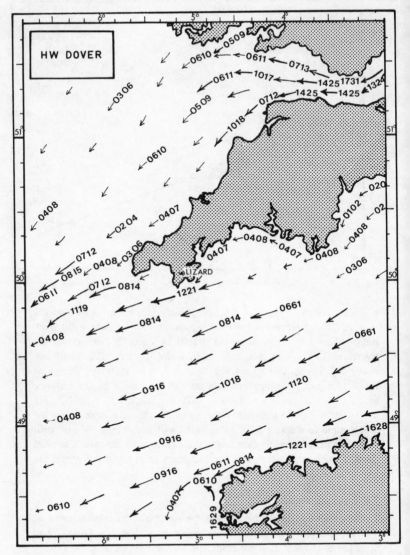

Fig. 23

may be seen; just south of the Lizard appear the figures '1221' between two arrows, and they mean that at this point when it is high water at Dover the tidal stream runs at an average speed of 1·2 knots at neaps and 2·1 knots at springs in the direction of the arrow – about 250°. Provided you have access to a Dover tide table, you can work out tidal set and rate for any hour of the day or night. Interpolation is made easy by a diagram inside the front cover, and reproduced here as figure 24, which you use by laying a ruler between one rate and the other and reading off the predicted figure by reference to the range of tide at Dover that day. In figure 24, if the mean range at Dover is 5 metres, a ruler laid from 1·2 knots to 2·1 knots will give a figure of 1·8 knots off the Lizard. Compass roses are not printed on the pages of *Admiralty Tidal Stream Atlases*, and you can either square the edge of the booklet with the edge of the chart and carry the direction across by parallel ruler or employ a protractor for the purpose.

Other methods of obtaining tidal information

The chartlets in *Reed's Nautical Almanac* and on Stanford's charts are used in the same way as the *Admiralty Tidal Stream Atlases*, although as they are smaller scale rather more care is needed. More general information appears in *Sailing Directions* in respect of stretches of coast and harbours. Here are two examples from the *West Coasts of England and Wales Pilot*:

'Tidal Streams.   The streams run mainly in the direction of the coast at a spring rate of from 1 to 2 knots. They are stronger off Cape Cornwall and Hartland Point, and off salient points, but weaker in the bays between. There is an indraught towards Bude Bay'.

and,

'Aberystwyth.   Tidal streams are generally weak. There is always a surface current setting out of the harbour at a rate of 1 knot on the flood stream to 3 knots on the ebb'.

Reed's Nautical Almanac contains useful tidal notes; here, for example, is an edited digest of information on anomalies at Shoreham:

'Within Shoreham Harbour the flood stream sets almost entirely up Western Arm with little change of rate except at the bottleneck off

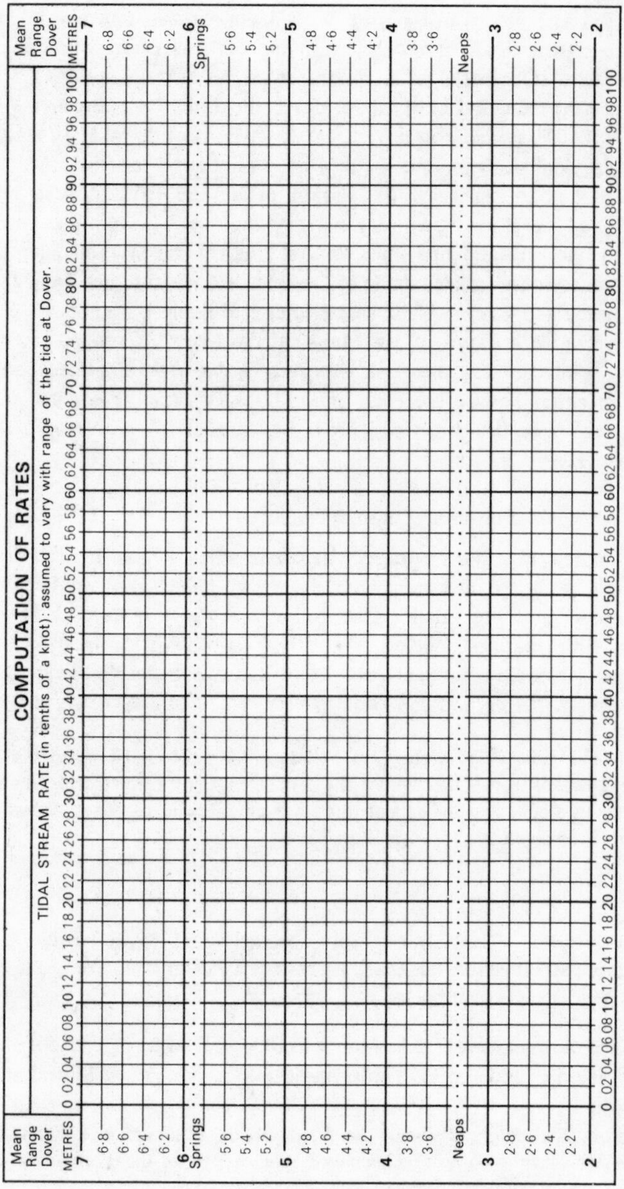

COMPUTATION OF RATES

TIDAL STREAM RATE (in tenths of a knot): assumed to vary with range of the tide at Dover.

Reproduced from Admiralty publication NP250 with the sanction of the Controller, HM Stationery Office and of the Hydrographer of the Navy.

Fig. 24

Soldiers Point where it attains a rate of 4 knots at Springs ... the ebb stream combined with the river current can attain a rate of 5 knots off Soldiers Point ... and the ebb stream from the harbour mouth overcomes the last of the west-going and the beginning of the east-going Channel streams which are therefore not felt until well clear of the Harbour'.

These quotations show that descriptive information can supplement the data obtained from tables and atlases – particularly when near the coast or in river entrances. You should also be prepared to work out the rate and set of tidal streams for yourself when necessary, and figure 25 illustrates one method of doing so.

To find tidal direction and rate

In figure 25 you are the navigator of a yacht out on a day sail, and you discover after casting off that the owner has left the tidal atlas in the boot of his car. As you pass the harbour beacon you observe that the tide appears to be setting south south-east at about 1 knot. How do you confirm this guess?

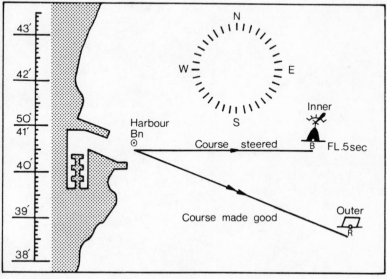

Fig. 25

The true course to make the Inner buoy is 090° and, resisting the temptation to steer for the mark, you direct the helmsman to steer the appropriate compass course to make good 090° T. What you are doing is ignoring the tide altogether, and you anticipate that at the end of a fixed period of time the difference in position between where you are and where you would have been had there been no tide will represent the tidal set and rate. Your speed is 4 knots, and after an hour you reach the Outer buoy. Two sides of the tidal triangle are shown in figure 25; you must supply the third. Try the following questions:

1. Were you right in estimating that the direction of the tide was south south-easterly?
2. What was the strength of the tide in one hour?
3. What true course (to the nearest 10°) should you have steered to make the Inner buoy?

(*Answers on page 118.*)

Chapter Four

The Compass

Two types of magnetic compasses are in use in small craft – the steering compass and the hand-bearing compass. The former is, or should be, fixed; the latter is portable and when not in use generally lives in a flexible rubber mounting near the navigator's berth. Steering compasses should be installed, if possible, on the centre line of a yacht and positioned as far away as possible from the engine or other large lumps of metal that are likely to increase compass error. If you have to install a steering compass off-centre always ensure by measurement that the lubber line or other fore-and-aft marking on the compass is parallel to the fore-and-aft line of the vessel. The steering compass should be so placed that the helmsman can read the card without craning his neck unduly, and it should have a light for night use. Its performance will be affected if bubbles form in the compass liquid, and it will then be necessary to turn it upside down, unscrew the bottom plug, and top it up with a 50/50 mixture of pure alcohol and distilled water, using an eyedropper. Figure 26 shows what the two types of compasses look like: they are subject to a total error with two components, and we will deal with variation first.

Variation

Variation arises because geographical north and magnetic north do not coincide, and the practical effect in British waters is that the north-seeking end of a compass needle or bar magnet points towards Hudson's Bay instead of the North Pole. Variation depends both on where you are at the time of taking observations and on the year in question; in western Europe it is a reducing figure and our fortunate grandchildren will be able to navigate for a year or two without allow-

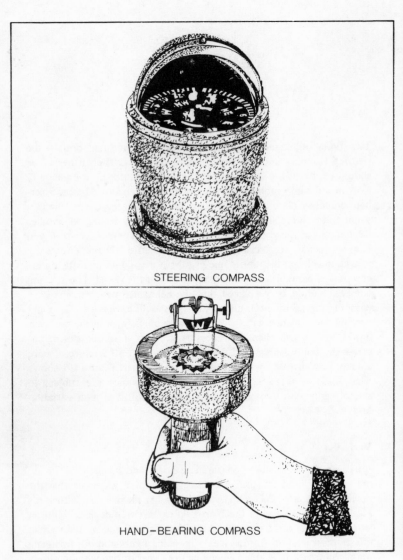

STEERING COMPASS

HAND–BEARING COMPASS

Fig. 26

ing for it. The amount of magnetic variation that has to be allowed for in a particular sea area is printed on charts along the horizontal bar of the inner ring of the compass rose, and the phrase may read, 'Variation 10° 50′ w (1966) decreasing 5′ annually' meaning that in 1976 you must allow 10°50′ minus 5 × 10 or 50 minutes to make it 10° westerly variation for the area where you are voyaging. True courses and bearings that have been adjusted for magnetic variation are termed magnetic courses and bearings, and as the plotting of true courses and bearings from magnetic ones is a large part of a navigator's work you must get it right from the start. Look at figure 27 and follow the reasoning.

Magnetic to true

The inner ring of the compass rose at the top of figure 27 tilts to the left, and the 10° divergence between True North and Magnetic North is the variation at our present position. In the lower half of the illustration the yacht is moving on a magnetic course of 060° with the needle of its deviation-free compass pointing, as it always does, to Magnetic North and the lubber line opposite the 060° marking on the compass card. We have to convert magnetic to true, and the rule is that when converting from a magnetic to a true course when the variation is westerly the amount of variation is subtracted.

There are several mnemonics for remembering how to convert courses and bearings. CADET is a popular — 'from compass to true add east' — and so is 'variation east, compass least, variation west, compass best', but I like the old coasting rhyme 'compass to true, signs do. True to compass, t'other way . . .' because the 'signs do' part treats east as plus and west as minus, and that is the way it looks on a compass rose. Do not worry about these mnemonics too much at this stage; we will go through the process diagramatically a few pages further on.

In this example the sum goes:

Magnetic Course	060°	('Compass to true, signs do',
Variation 10° W	−10°	which makes W variation −)
True Course	050°	

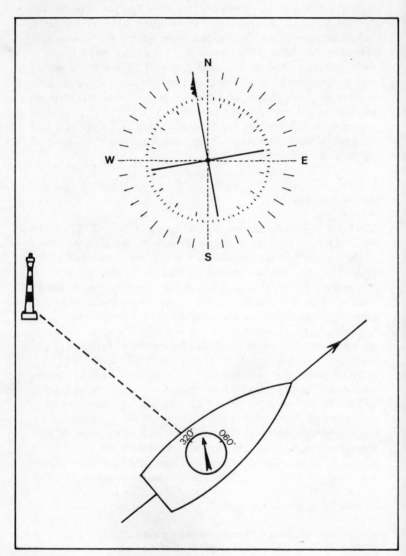

Fig. 27

Let us do it once more. A lighthouse on the port quarter bears 320°
by a deviation-free hand-bearing compass, and the sum goes:

Magnetic Bearing	320°	('Compass to true, signs do',
Variation 10° W	−10°	which makes W variation −)
True Bearing	310°	

If you still have any lingering doubts about converting from magnetic
to true, try using a parallel ruler on figure 27 and carry the magnetic
course and the magnetic bearing over to the compass rose, count-
ing round the outer ring in 10° steps from true north to be sure the
sum is right.

Deviation

Deviation is that second part of total compass error that cannot be
ascribed to variation, and if you think the definition woolly it is
necessarily so because deviation has so many causes. It may reflect
the direction the yacht lay in the earth's magnetic field as it was being
built, the hammering it got in a gale, the effect on the compass of a
minor electrical circuit or the sum of the magnetic attractions of tools
or tins in the bilges. Deviation includes all magnetic influences, except
variation, and arises because the compass needle, like any other
metallic object, is affected by the force lines of a boat's magnetic
field, and it alters with the direction of the ship's head. This is the
crucial difference between variation and deviation − variation
depends on where you are in the earth's magnetic field (your position)
and is the same for all craft in any one area; deviation alters from
boat to boat (and from compass to compass in any one boat) and
depends also on the ship's heading at the moment you consult the
compass. Professional compass adjusters can tame recalcitrant compasses with magnets to reduce excessive deviation, and then supply
deviation cards looking something like the table, top of page
58.

These cards are customarily pinned up over the chart table for easy
reference, and may be more, or less, detailed. Warships will carry
tables giving the deviation for every 10°, merchant vessels are more
likely to work on a figure of 20° and sailing yachts will often be

Table of Deviations		
Ship's Head Compass	Deviation	Ship's Head Magnetic
000°	4E	004°
020°	2E	022°
040°	2W	038°
060	4W	056°
080°	6W	074°
100°	7W	093°
120°	7W	113°
140°	7W	133°
160°	6W	154°
180°	4W	176°
200°	2W	198°
220°	1E	221°
240°	2E	242°
260°	4E	264°
280°	5E	285°
300°	6E	306°
320°	6E	326°
340°	5E	345°
360°	4E	004°

content to record the deviation for the eight principal points of the compass. No matter, the principle is the same, and as they are most commonly used in converting compass courses and bearings to true courses and bearings that aspect of their use will be tackled first.

Compass to true

Total compass error is made up of variation and deviation, and the conversion of compass courses and bearings is correspondingly in two stages. Imagine that you are sailing along on a compass course of 240° and wish to plot it as a true course. 240° in column 1 of the table on this page gives a deviation of 2° E in column 2, and the calculation begins:

Compass Course	240°	('Compass to true, signs do',
Deviation 2° E	+2°	which makes E deviation +)
	——	
Magnetic Course	242°	
	——	

Now apply the variation, which from the chart is 10° w:

Magnetic Course	242°	('Compass to true, signs do',
Variation 10° W	−10°	which makes W variation −)
True Course	232°	

Try the following for yourself, using the deviation table on page 58 and a variation of 10° w:

	Compass Course	Deviation	Magnetic Course	Variation	True Course
1.	340°				
2.	250°				
3.	030°				

(*Answers on page 118.*)

Did you interpolate correctly? The deviation figure for 250° ship's head by compass is 3° E, and that for 030° ship's head by compass is nil. When converting bearings, the deviation correction is applied to the bearing on the basis of the ship's head at the time. An example. You are sailing on a compass course of 180° when you take the bearings of a beacon and a lighthouse as 123° and 201° respectively. The deviation table gives 4° w as the deviation on a 180° heading, and your calculations go:

Beacon		Lighthouse	
Compass Bearing	123°	Compass Bearing	201°
Deviation 4° W	−4°	Deviation	−4°
Magnetic Bearing	119°	Magnetic Bearing	197°
Variation 10° W	−10	Variation	−10°
True Bearing	109°	True Bearing	187°

Total compass error

From this last example you may see that total compass error is 14° w, and there are advantages sometimes in dealing with variation and deviation as one figure. When taking a series of bearings on a steady course, for example, the total figure can be added or subtracted mentally and true bearings plotted quickly, while where variation and deviation are of different names and tend to cancel out, or nearly do so, it is better to use a total figure. The rule for calculating total compass error is:

Same name *add* and name the same;
Different name *subtract* and name as the greater.

Thus, 10° w variation and 4° w deviation are added and give a total compass error of 14° w: 10° w variation and 8° E deviation are subtracted to give a total compass error of 2° w.

True to compass

Here we reverse the order of work and apply the variation before the deviation. The third column in the deviation table comes into the picture and gives the deviation figure because column 1, ship's head by compass is not known and, as far as course-setting is concerned, is what we are seeking to establish. Let us start by reversing the example on page 58 by converting a true course of 232° to a compass course:

True Course	232°	('True to compass, t'other way',
Variation 10° W	+10°	which makes W variation +)
Magnetic Course	242°	
Deviation 2E	−2°	(Found from the 242° figure
	———	in column 3 of the table)
Compass Course	240°	

Answer the following, using the deviation table on page 58 and taking the variation as 10° w.

	True Course	Variation	Magnetic Course	Deviation	Compass Course
1.	166°				
2.	243°				
3.	177°				

(*Answers on page 118.*)

The diagram method

If in any doubt, draw a picture. Figure 28 outlines a typical situation. A yacht is bound from Port Hero to Seatown and the true course is 090°. The variation in this part of the world is 5° w and the deviation is 20° E. You put yourself on board facing forward and say to yourself: true course to find compass course – apply westerly variation and deviation to the right and easterly deviation and variation to the left. Then draw in 5° of variation to the right of the true course line and label it 'Magnetic' to avoid confusion. Repeat the formula again – 'true course to find compass course ... easterly deviation and variation to the left' – and draw in the third line 20° to the left of the second, labelling it 'Compass'. The compass course to steer is 075°. The full formula is:

True Course to find Compass Course

Apply *westerly* variation and deviation to the *right*
Apply *easterly* variation and deviation to the *left*

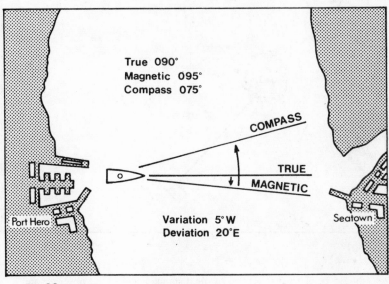

Fig. 28

Compass Course to find True Course

Apply *westerly* variation and deviation to the *left*
Apply *easterly* variation and deviation to the *right*

Finding the deviation

The deviation cards are sometimes mislaid and sometimes grow very inaccurate so that you have to work out a new table, but the prospect need cause no alarm. The quickest method is to get a true line of bearing from a transit of two charted shore objects and obtain the total compass error on various headings.

(a) *Transit method*

The selected shore marks should have sharply-defined vertical edges so as to correspond neatly when in line, and the most distant mark

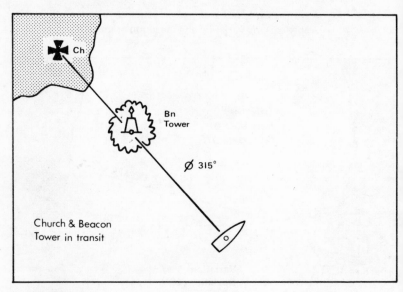

Fig. 29

should be at least one-third of the distance between the observer and the nearest mark. A transit is depicted in figure 29 where a church and beacon in line give the observer to seaward a line of true bearing of 315°. Calm conditions are essential, and the yacht is sailed slowly to and fro over the line of transit with its head held briefly on the headings required. Note the compass bearing as the marks come

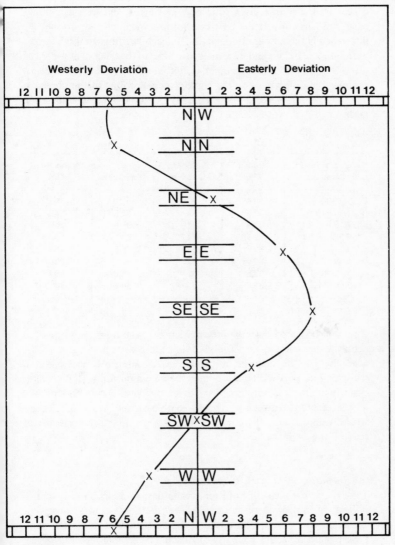

Fig. 30

exactly in line. The difference between 315° and the compass reading of the transit marks gives total compass error, but to make things easy you can convert the true bearing to a magnetic one so that the difference is the amount of deviation on each heading. In this case the variation is 10° w and the magnetic line of bearing will be 315° plus 10°, makes 325° magnetic. For simplicity, the table below outlines the differences on the eight principal points of the compass, and columns, 1, 4 and 5 will eventually be employed as the deviation table.

Ship's Head Compass	Transit (M)	Compass Bearing	Deviation	Ship's Head (M)
N (000°)	325°	330 °	5 ° W	355°
NE (045°)	325°	324°	1° E	046°
E (090°)	325°	319°	6° E	096°
SE (135°)	325°	317°	8° E	143°
S (180°)	325°	321°	4° E	184°
SW (225°)	325°	325°	Nil	225°
W (270°)	325°	328°	3° W	267°
NW (315°)	325°	331°	6° W	309°

You may prefer to have the information in visual form, and figure 30 shows a deviation diagram embodying these deviation figures. One advantage of the diagram is that it makes interpolation easier. If, for example, you wanted to obtain the deviation for a south south-easterly course it is only necessary to lay the parallel rule horizontally on the diagram between south and south-east, making a light pencil stroke where it cuts the curve, and then align the ruler vertically to read off the deviation as 7° E.

(b) *Deviation by bearing of distant object*
Take the yacht well offshore on a calm day so as to be at least five miles from a prominent mark on shore, such as a church spire. Put the yacht round in a tight circle, stopping long enough for the compass needle to settle properly on each of the main points of the compass to note the bearing of the spire. Add all the values together and divide by eight, as follows:

Ship's head by compass	Compass bearing of spire
N	186°
NE	179°
E	174°
SE	172°
S	176°
SW	180°
W	183°
NW	186°
	8)1,436

Mean figure   179·5°

This mean or average figure is a useful check on accuracy, because the correct magnetic bearing of the spire is 180°, and we can now work out the individual deviations:

Ship's head compass	Spire (M)	Spire (C)	Sum	Deviation
N	180°	186°	+6	6° W
NE	180°	179°	−1	1° E
E	180°	174°	−6	6° E
SE	180°	172°	−8	8° E
S	180°	176°	−4	4° E
SW	180°	180°	0	Nil
W	180°	183°	+3	3° W
NW	180°	186°	+6	6° W

Use of the hand-bearing compass

The hand-bearer can be used anywhere on the yacht, although it is good practice to avoid positions where metal can influence the reading and, as far as possible, to take bearings from the same spot for which any deviation may be known and is recorded on its own deviation card. A good all-round view is essential, and the compass should be held with the bowl horizontal until the card stops swinging. Line up the compass so that your eye and the object observed and the dot, notch or hairline make a straight line, looking over or under the reflecting prism as circumstances demand. Figure 31 shows a church spire bearing 179° by hand-bearer: the yacht is on a south-easterly

Fig. 31

course and, using the deviation diagram in figure 30, find the true
bearing if the variation is 10° w. (*Answer on page 118.*)

The amplitude method

When out of sight of land the navigator is able to check his deviation
on an easterly or westerly course by reference to the sun's true bearing at sunrise and sunset, and all he requires to do so is a current
copy of *Reed's Nautical Almanac* and knowledge of his approximate
latitude. The amplitude method, as it is called, rests on getting the
sun's bearing by compass when it is half its diameter above the
horizon – as demonstrated in figure 32 – and in this example a yacht
is steering 280° off Dungeness in latitude 51° N just before sunset
on the 21st August. The navigator takes the sun's bearing as it sets
and gets 289° by compass. The fourth monthly page in *Reed's
Nautical Almanac* for August shows the sun's declination as from
12° 13·6′ N to 11° 55·3′ N, but we only want a whole number and
settle for 12° N. The table of sun's true bearing at sunrise and sunset

is entered with this 12° declination at the top and the 51° latitude down the side; the appropriate entry reads 70·7°. Following the rule printed beneath the table '...name the bearing the same as the declination north or south; and east if rising, west if setting...', the sun's true bearing is N 70·7° W or 289·3°. To the nearest degree this is 289°, and we have:

Sun's true bearing	289°
Compass bearing	289°
Total Compass Error	0
but, Variation is	6° W

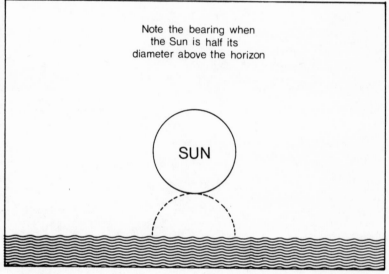

Note the bearing when the Sun is half its diameter above the horizon

SUN

Fig. 32

Therefore the deviation when the yacht is on a 280° heading must be 6° E. The deviation table on page 58 shows a deviation of 5° E for a 280° heading? Is this a sufficient discrepancy to justify altering the table? No, it can be noted in the log, but you would need further evidence in the form of other departures from the table on other headings before you began to doubt the validity of the figures.

A last word

The most important thing to remember from this chapter is that variation and deviation are both dependent variables; variation depending on position on the sea and deviation on the direction of the ship's head at the time of using the compass. Grasp that and you will never err in handling compass error.

Chapter Five

Position and Position Lines

A navigator spends most of his time answering two questions – where am I now? which way do I go next? – and this chapter is all about the first question, the problem of position. In global terms, we express position by means of latitude and longitude, the angular distance north or south of the equator, or east and west of Greenwich, measured from the centre of the earth.

Look at figure 33. O is the centre of an earth made of glass, WXE represents the plane of the equator and NYXS the plane of the Greenwich meridian so that the earth is quartered like an apple. An observer at the centre of the earth standing on the plane of the equator and looking towards Y would register an angle of 40° and if he shifted round to stand on the plane of Greenwich and looked towards Z he would register an angle of 74°. Any place on the same latitude as Y would also register as 40° and on the same longitude as Z as 74° when viewed from the earth's centre. The Statue of Liberty is therefore some 40° north of the equator and 74° west of Greenwich, and in the bottom half of figure 33 the position of the Statue of Liberty in New York is described in terms of latitude and longitude and plotted on a Mercator projection. The latitude always comes first so that the first half of New York's position description is 40° 28′ N and the second half is 73° 50′ W. Greenwich Observatory, which is on the Greenwich meridian, can have no longitude and its position description is 51° 29′ N 0° 0′. The positions of Port Said, Rio de Janeiro and Durban are given so that you can see that Port Said has a north and east position description, Durban is south and east, and Rio de Janeiro south and west.

Plotting position on the chart

So much for well-defined positions; now to plot a yacht's position on a chart. Look at the two parts of figure 34: we want to plot the present

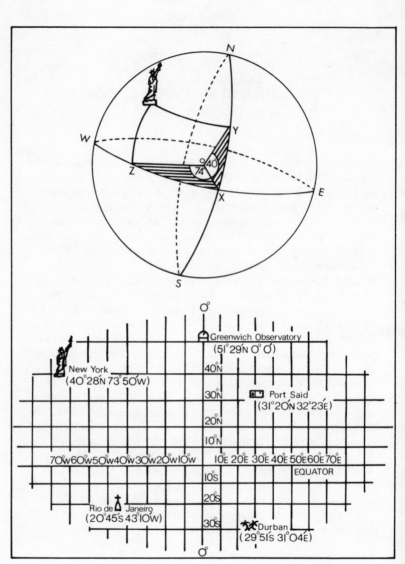

Fig. 33

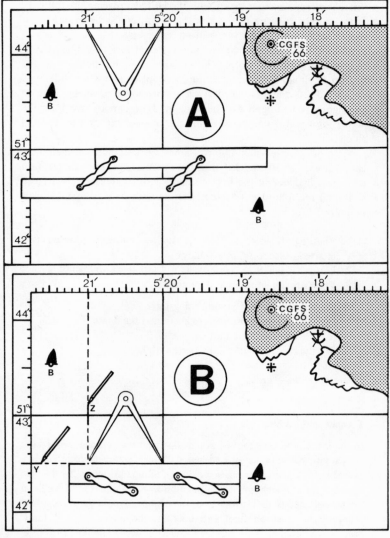

Fig. 34

position of a yacht at 51°42·5′ N, 5°21′ W, having just moved onto
this chart from another. Start with the latitude, placing the top edge
of the parallel ruler on the nearest line of latitude and reaching down
the latitude scale until the bottom edge cuts 51°42·5′ halfway
between the 42′ and 51°43′ markings. Pencil in a light line as at Y
in the lower part of figure 26, and then take the dividers to the
nearest meridian to the desired longitude, pricking off the difference
between 5°20′ and 21′ and carrying it down to the parallel of latitude
and lightly pencilling in Z. (The pencil markings are to save doing the
whole job again if you make a mistake transferring data by parallel
ruler.)

With the parallel ruler aligned on 51°42·5′ N, mark off the difference between 5°20′ and 21′ with the dividers and enter the position
as a pencilled dot in the first instance. Plotting position is a basic
skill, and the following problems can be answered using either half
of figure 34:

1. Plot 51°42·9′ N, 5°20·1′ W. It lies midway between two
    charted objects. What are they?
2. Plot 51°43·6′ N, 5°18·2′ W. Is it a safe place to anchor?
3. What are the latitudes and longitudes of:

    (a) the Coastguard Station's flagstaff?
    (b) the barely submerged rock south of the flagstaff?
    (c) the conical black buoy, top left?
    (d) the conical black buoy, bottom right?

(*Answers on page 118.*)

Transits and leading lights

In the last chapter we looked at transits from the compass correction
standpoint, but another look at figure 29 may persuade you that they
can also be a valuable aid in position-finding. In figure 29 the two
charted shore objects provide a position line running 135° true from
the beacon, and with knowledge of the distance from that mark, or by
crossing the position line with another, the navigator will know
exactly where he is. You may be wondering where the figure of 135°
true just quoted comes from: it is the reciprocal (or opposite) of
315°, for while the two marks bear 315° from the yacht it bears

315° minus 180°, making 135°, from the beacon and church in line.

A special case in the transit category is that of leading lights whose function is to guide vessels safely into port at night. Figure 35 shows a vessel approaching at night; it has only to keep the three

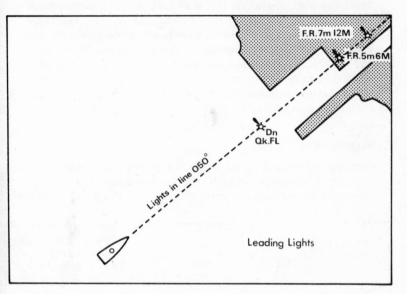

Fig. 35

lights in line – to keep on the transit – and will thereby follow the right track into harbour. The chart gives the light characteristics and the angle of approach; the appropriate volume of *Sailing Directions* will contain an entry reading something like this:

> Leading lights are exhibited, the front light from a red and white stone tower on Merchants Quay and the rear light from an openwork iron structure situated two cables NE. A light is exhibited from a dolphin 4 cables in front of the leading light tower on the same alignment.

The clearing line

A clearing line is, as the name implies, a method of keeping clear of danger by reference to shoremarks. The information is on the chart

at the seaward end of such lines, and a typical entry on a chart for
Start Bay reads, 'West end of trees over Widdecomb House in line
with the Northern White House in Beesands 321° clears south end of
the Skerries' and for yachts approaching Start Bay from the south-
ward and wishing to squeeze in between Skerries Bank and Start
Point this kind of position line is of great value. A more general
clearing line for Torbay is, 'Hopes Nose open of Berry Head true
north clears all dangers between Berry Head and the Mewstone' and
assists the northbound yacht making for Teignmouth. Older charts
and the *Cruising Association Handbook* contain numerous examples
of clearing lines for use close inshore, and in very confined waters
they are easier to follow than compass courses or shouted directions
from a lookout up forward.

Sectored lights

Although primarily designed for another purpose, the sectored light
can give a reasonably accurate position line at night. Figure 36
depicts an Isophase shore light with green, white and red sectors.

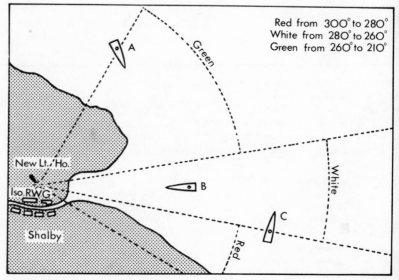

Fig. 36

The white sector gives the safe line of approach for big ships, while the red and green sectors indicate both that the approaching vessel is on an unsafe course and that it is too far over to starboard when it sees the green light and too far to port when it sees the red one. In figure 36 yacht 'A' has just begun to see the green light and her navigator will plot the true bearing of Shalby New Lighthouse as 210°. Yacht 'C' is passing from the red to the white sector and may record a true bearing from seaward of 280°. Yacht 'B' is making an orthodox approach in the white sector and is clear of all danger so long as the colour of the light does not change.

Position by depth contour line

A depth contour line may sometimes serve as a position line, particularly when the seabed shelves steeply and a yacht is crossing at right angles. Depth information comes from two sources, the echo sounder and by lead and line; let me deal with echo sounders first.

These useful little machines have a transmitter in the yacht sending sonic impulses downwards to the seabed and bouncing back to be received on a plate or transducer connected to a receiver. The time between transmission of the signal and receipt of the echo is proportional to the depth of water and when translated into feet, fathoms or metres, is reproduced on a dial. Two small corrections have to be applied to get the depth right; one for the height of tide above chart datum at the time of taking the sounding and another for the difference between water level and the transmitter and transducer in the hull.

An example. You are bound from Burnham to Dunkirk and by your reckoning about to cross the Sandettie Bank at right angles. The chart shows a sudden rise in the seabed at this point and it is about the time of high water at Dunkirk. Your echo sounder, which transmits and receives 3 feet below the waterline, is switched on and after registering 21 fathoms for a while suddenly falls to 12 fathoms. You note the time and work out the correct depth of water. *Reed's Nautical Almanac* tells you that high water at Dunkirk today gives 5·5 metres above chart datum, and the conversion table that 5·5 metres is 3 fathoms. Take away 3 fathoms from 12 and you get 9; add half a fathom for the 3 feet difference between transducer and water level and the corrected sounding is 9½ fathoms. Does this square with the chart? Yes, this is consistent with the charted depth at the northern end of the Sandettie Bank and you can draw in a position line coinciding with the north-western edge of the shoal and enter the time alongside it.

One word of caution about echo sounders. They occasionally give a second trace echo because the signal bounces twice off the seabed and records double the correct depth, but you will observe that the signal is much weaker than usual and will fade if sensitivity is reduced. False echoes from shoals of fish, seaweed or plankton may appear on those types of depth recorders producing paper traces, but the dial type commonly fitted in yachts is less likely to be affected.

Every yacht should carry a lead and line, and while the lead can be purchased at the chandlers it is usually necessary to prepare the line and put in the marks yourself. Start with 140 feet of good quality codline, soak it and dry it several times and then rub it with candle grease. Put in the marks as demonstrated in figure 37; the one-fathom mark is optional, and the different materials used are so that you may ascertain the depth by feel at night. To use the lead, stand up by the shrouds with an arm round one of them and wearing a safety harness clipped on round the mast. Swing the lead with a scope of

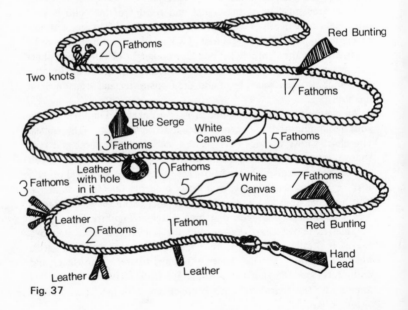

Fig. 37

four or five feet and cast it well ahead, letting the line run through your fingers until you feel the lead bump on the bottom. Note the nearest mark when the line is vertical and recover the line hand over hand. As before, the figure obtained will have to be adjusted for height of tide above chart datum and there will be an additional correction for the difference between the mark and sea level. If you would prefer to put in metric marks on your lead line, they are as follows:

metres	mark	metres
1	one strip of leather	11
2	two strips of leather	12
3	blue bunting	13
4	green and white bunting	14
5	white bunting	15
6	green bunting	16
7	red bunting	17
8	blue and white bunting	18
9	red and white bunting	19
10	piece of leather with hole	20

Position from a line of soundings

In thick weather a line of soundings may give an excellent position line when contrasted with charted depths, and the process is illustrated in figure 38. The navigator of the boat at the top of the drawing is approaching land in poor visibility, and directing the taking of soundings at fixed intervals. He knows his speed from the log, and plots the depths obtained and suitably corrected on a piece of paper to the same scale as the chart. He moves the piece of paper around on the chart, keeping the marked edge parallel to his true course, until the soundings match. In figure 38 he has just made the match: it tells him that he is clear of the dangerous headland marked 'B' on his present course, and a prolongation of the straight edge of his strip of paper is a position line on which he must be. This technique works best when there is a steady increase or decrease in depth; it is not effective on steep-to coasts or where there is little variation in depth over long distances.

A final exercise

Take out your old chart and search for transits, clearing lines or sectored lights likely to be useful to the navigator. Then use your

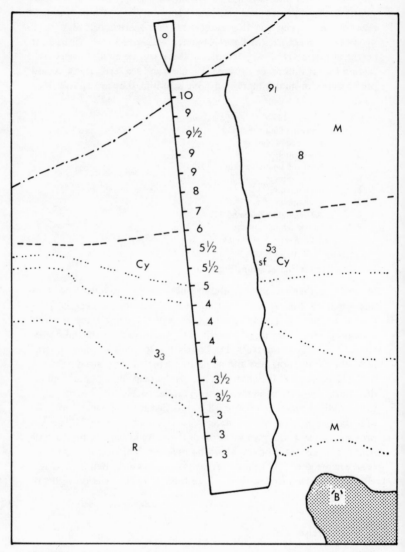

Fig. 38

parallel ruler and dividers to find the latitude and longitude of all the lighthouses on it, comparing your answers with their positions as recorded in the appropriate volume of *Sailing Directions*. End by trying the following questions:

1. What is the reciprocal of 010°?
2. On a hand lead line, what is the mark for 10 fathoms?
3. On a hand lead line, what is the mark for 12 metres?
4. Turn back to figure 13 on page 27. What are the latitudes of:
   (a) the 1315 hours fixed position?
   (b) the 1330 hours fixed position?
   (c) position 'A'?

(Answers on page 118.)

Chapter Six

Fixes

Navigators are a suspicious race, and rightly so. Tidal calculations are based on estimates, compasses are erratic and rain squalls, fog or mist soon make a nonsense of dead reckoning. Consequently, a navigator fixes his position by reference to shore objects whenever he can, using cross-bearings, the running fix, the four-point bearing, distance off tables, vertical and horizontal sextant angles and radio aids for the purpose. Let us look at each in turn, starting with the cross-bearing.

Cross-bearings

Look at the top half of figure 39. The yacht is passing an island on its north side and the beacon on the eastern end, the church and the lighthouse are in clear view. The navigator takes the bearing of each in quick succession and converts the compass readings to:

Beacon	132° T
Spire	161° T
Lighthouse	212° T

He plots them on the chart, draws a circle around the meeting point to indicate a fixed position and enters the time alongside. Ideally, the angle of 'cut' should be 30° between bearings and the central object should be the closest. However, these considerations should not confine you too much – the angle between the beacon and spire in figure 39 is less than 30° but, as a three-line fix is always superior to a two-line fix, the third line of bearing is a useful check on accuracy. If only two objects are available a 'cut' at right angles gives the best results. If the three lines do not meet at a point you get a 'cocked hat' or small triangle; a large 'cocked hat' may indicate

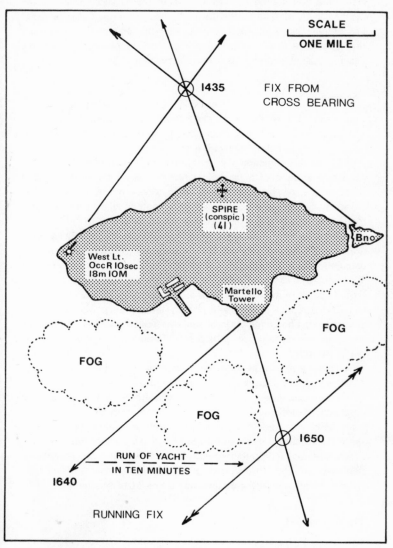

Fig. 39

error and you should try again, a small one is acceptable and the centre can be marked with a dot and given fix status. Cross-bearings are simple to take and easy to plot; after the chartwork is finished a note should be made in the rough log or on the plotting sheet of the bearings, the objects employed and the time.

The running fix

The lower part of figure 39 deals with the running fix, and this technique comes into play when, by reason of restricted visibility or distance, only one shore object is available.

At 1640 the navigator of an eastbound yacht travelling at 12 knots catches a glimpse of a martello tower broad on the port bow and takes a bearing by hand-bearer that works out as 048° T. Fog closes in, but ten minutes later he gets another glimpse of the same tower and snaps a second bearing which converts to 347° T. He plots both of them, adding a single arrowhead to show what they are at the seaward ends of the lines of bearing. A quick mental calculation tells him that in ten minutes a motor yacht travelling at 12 knots will cover 2 miles, and he steps off two miles from the latitude scale in an 090° direction and draws in by parallel ruler a transferred replica of the 1640 position line, adding two arrowheads at each end. The conjunction of this transferred position line and the 1650 line of bearing gives a fix for 1650, and that time is entered as the fix is circled.

A running fix can be valuable at night when a single light on the coast is the sole data available, but in tidal waters you have to be careful in calculating the 'run' between observations. It may be necessary to plot a tidal triangle to get the 'run' right or to add or sub-tract the effect of tide when it is fair or foul. In sailing yachts, where speed is not constant, a careful reading of the log between observations is essential. Remember your arrowheads: one for a bearing or position line; two for a transferred bearing or transferred position line. Do you recall what three arrowheads means? (*Answer on page 119.*)

The four-point bearing

This method depends on knowledge of the relative angles between the object and the fore-and-aft line of the ship. In figure 40 the log reading is noted when the object bears four points (45°) relative to the fore-and-aft line, and again when it is abeam (at 90° to the fore-and-aft line). By the magic of mathematics the distance run equals the distance off. There is no need to plot the first bearing, but by plotting the second bearing you get a position line and a distance off equal to the run of the ship. When coasting it is common practice to alter course off headlands, and if the four-point bearing method is used a reliable fix can be obtained from which to set the next leg of the voyage. Doubling the angle on the bow is a variant of the four-point bearing, and it has the further advantage that you do not have to wait until the object is abeam.

In the top half of figure 41 the principle is explained. At 1400 Spen Light bears 30° on the starboard bow, and at 1430 it bears 60°. Provided that course and speed are maintained, and that leeway and tidal streams are negligible, the distance off will equal the distance run. By also noting the log reading when the light bears 45° you get a second chance of a fix, and if conditions are favourable it is good practice to try both methods, thus getting two distances off and two fixes for little effort from one charted feature. This range and bearing principle is also pertinent to the next example.

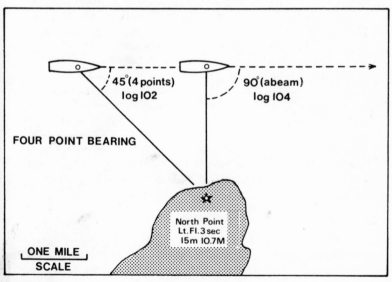

Fig. 40

Distance off by tables

Burton's Nautical Tables, *Norie's Tables*, the *Admiralty List of Lights and Fog Signals* and *Reed's Nautical Almanac* all contain tables based on the curvature of the earth which give the geographical ranges of lights relative to the height of the light and the height of the eye of the observer, and thus the distance between them. This type of poor man's rangefinder is easy to operate, and a fragment of a simple table is reproduced at the foot of figure 41. The situation in the centre of figure 41 is that an observer in a yacht whose height of eye is four metres begins to get a constant view of Spen Light on a true bearing of 030° and the chart shows that the lantern is 24 metres above Mean Higher High Water. By entering the table with his height of eye at the top and the height of the light at the left he finds that the distance off is 14 miles. The reciprocal of 030° is 210° and the observer may plot a line of bearing 210° T from Spen Light, step off 14 miles from the latitude scale and circle the fixed position.

The tables are useful, but may mislead. In very clear weather when a uniform layer of cloud covers the sky you may see lights reflected from the underside of the layer and apparently visible although actually still below the horizon. Mirages sometimes enlarge distant objects, and at sunset lights are briefly seen at greater than normal distances. The 'loom' or fuzzy reflection of a light should not be mistaken for the light itself, and the only way to tell which is which is to bob up and down to be sure that what you are seeing is the twinkle of the light rather than the glow of the 'loom'. Self-deception is another problem, for there always seems to be a tendency at night to make the flash pattern of a distant light fit that of a light you are expecting to see. The only remedy is to count the characteristics out loud to yourself several times, resisting the impulse to rush to the chart, almanac or the appropriate volume of the *Admiralty List of Lights and Fog Signals* to confirm any first wild guesses.

Distance off by vertical sextant angle

This simple method for keeping clear of dangers by remaining on a curved position line deserves to be better known, and all the information you need is the charted height of the object and the distance off you wish to maintain.

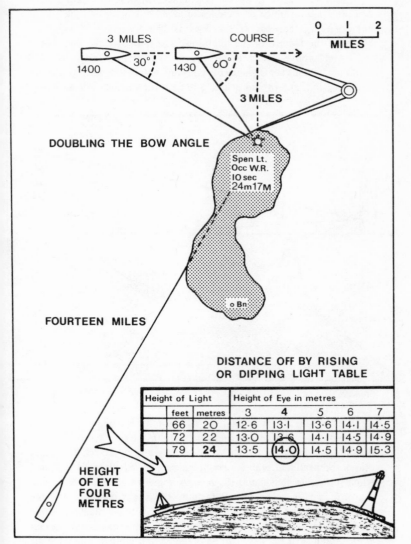

0 1 2
MILES

3 MILES

COURSE

1400 30° 1430 60°

3 MILES

DOUBLING THE BOW ANGLE

Spen Lt.
Occ W.R.
IO sec
24m 17M

FOURTEEN MILES

o Bn

**DISTANCE OFF BY RISING
OR DIPPING LIGHT TABLE**

Height of Light		Height of Eye in metres				
feet	metres	3	4	5	6	7
66	20	12·6	13·1	13·6	14·1	14·5
72	22	13·0	13·6	14·1	14·5	14·9
79	**24**	13·5	(14·0)	14·5	14·9	15·3

**HEIGHT
OF EYE
FOUR
METRES**

Fig. 41

Figure 42 illustrates the case of a yacht wishing to round a head-land at a safe distance of 4 cables to avoid a dangerous rock and fix her position accurately as she does so. The navigator looks up the height of the lantern of the lighthouse and finds it to be 198 metres (650 feet) above Mean Higher High Water. In *Reed's Nautical Almanac* he finds the distance off table and enters it at the top with the height of the lantern and at the side with the distance off he wishes

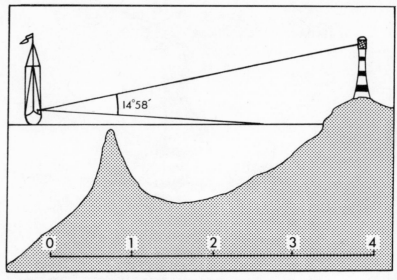

Fig. 42

to be, extracting a sextant angle of 14° 58′ from the body of the table. He begins taking the sextant angle between the lantern and the shore — obtaining an image in the telescope as shown in figure 43. The yacht closes the headland with a sextant reading of less than 14° 58′, and when it reaches that figure the navigator gives orders to bear off to seaward. So, in an on-and-off fashion, the yacht curves round the headland, keeping at least 4 cables distant. Another member of the crew can be taking bearings while the navigator takes the sextant angle, and a series of fixes can be obtained and plotted. The table for distance off by vertical sextant angle can also be used in the same way as that for distance off by dipping lights, entering it with the

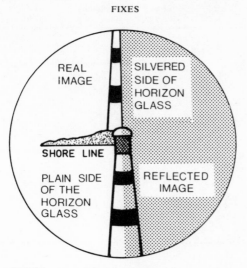

Fig. 43

sextant angle and the height of the charted object to get the distance and plotting on a bearing and range basis. No allowance is made in the vertical sextant angle table for height of eye or height of tide, and the distance obtained will be a minimum rather than a maximum figure.

Use of horizontal sextant angle

In settled summer weather, very accurate fixes can be obtained from distant objects by using the sextant and compass together. In figure 44 a navigator whose yacht is about 12 miles offshore has taken the bearing of the lighthouse as 270° True. Due to his distance offshore, he cannot get a 30° 'cut' with another shore object, but there is a church quite close to the lighthouse and he takes the angle between the church and lighthouse by sextant as 15°00′. Drawing in the true line of bearing to the lighthouse, he then puts in a second line of bearing at a 15° angle anywhere along it – in figure 44 it is marked 'A'. Then, using the parallel ruler, he transfers 'A' until such time as it passes through the church, drawing in the transferred line of bearing 'B' and marking the fix. The only difficulty likely to be experienced is in using the sextant at an unfamiliar angle, and the best way of doing it is to hold the instrument in your right hand and push the

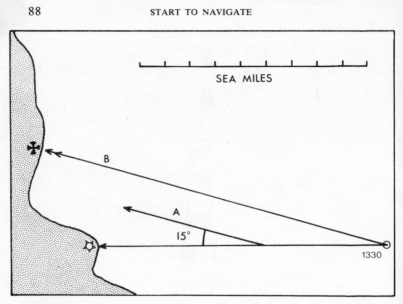

Fig. 44

index forward with your left, swivelling the instrument to the right as the reflected image moves left, and make the fine adjustment after the images roughly coincide. It sounds complicated, but a little practice on a calm day will confirm how easy it is.

Radio aids

As I said earlier, navigators are a suspicious race, and as far as radio aids are concerned their suspicions are fully justified. In theory, direction-finding by reference to shore-based marine and aeronautical radiobeacons should be foolproof, and we will go through it as though it were so before dealing with the snags and difficulties and listing all the reservations as to accuracy and reliability.

United Kingdom waters are richly supplied with radiobeacons, and any one, two, three or four position lines obtained from them can be plotted to obtain fixes in the same way as cross-bearings of objects on shore. The first step is to find beacons appropriate for use at your present position, and this can be done in three ways. An exami-

nation of the chart will reveal magenta (mauve) circles with the letters
RC, R♀ B♫ or 'Aero RC' marking the whereabouts of beacons, or you
can search in Vol. 2 of the *Admiralty List of Radio Signals* or in
Reed's Nautical Almanac where there are quick-reference maps
giving their physical location.

As an example we will assume that a yacht is crossing from Wey-
mouth to Alderney and is about fifteen miles from her destination
when visibility deteriorates. The first obvious choice of beacon is the
one on the Casquets which transmits:

Signal	Meaning
QS,QS,QS,QS	Station identification
A long dash taking 25 seconds	To obtain the null – see below
QS,QS (— — · — · · ·)	Further station identification
Silence for 5 seconds	Gap before another station transmits

for one minute every six minutes on 298·8 kHz. Casquets is part of
the Channel West group of beacons, and the important part of the
signal is the 25-second dash of continuous transmission. While the
dash is heard you have to rotate the aerial or hand-held part of the set
to get the silent null. With loop aerials the figure of bearing
obtained is relative to the fore-and-aft line of the ship and with hand-
held sets with ferrite rods an allowance is made for deviation, but you
should eventually get a true line of bearing to plot on the chart.
Pointe de Barfleur on 291·9 kHz is suitable for the next position line,
and the third can be Alderney aeronautical radiobeacon which transmits ALD and long dashes on 383 kHz. In each case you will be
seeking the null – the silent spot – and to get it accurately it is best to
rotate the set from where you just hear the dash to where you next
just hear the dash, note the extremities of the null and take the figure
in the middle. Over short distances – and that means less than 25
miles – quite good results can be obtained without the need for
complicated corrections, but over that distance your difficulties
increase. Let us now deal with them.

Quadrantal error is the first problem; it is caused by steel wire
rigging acting as an aerial and distorting the direction of the signal.
Insulation is one answer, but much depends on the initial installation
of the set. Loop aerials should be fitted at a height on the centre line
of the ship and the set placed so as to avoid possible interference
from other electrical apparatus, while portable receivers such as the
'Homer/Heron' and 'Seafix' types are best used out on deck and well

away from standing rigging. If quadrantal error exists, it is allowed for in the same way as deviation and corrected from a calibration card of readings on different relative headings.

Half-convergency is another possible source of error in the bearing received; it arises because radio signals follow a curved great circle path while bearings on a chart are rhumb lines. Fortunately, a correction is only required for more distant signals, and by sticking to a 25-mile limit of reliability for radiobeacons it can be ignored.

Coastal refraction is a distortion of the signal that occurs when the transmitter and the coast are at a narrow angle from your position, and sky-wave effects resulting from the signal reflecting from the ionosphere blur the null at night and are particularly troublesome around dawn and dusk. Again, a 25-mile limit is the cure for sky-wave errors: coastal refraction is at its greatest when the signal path is almost parallel to a high shore, and the answer is to find another station.

The listed ranges of radiobeacons should always be regarded with healthy scepticism, and although aerobeacons may often be picked up at great distances the signal has probably passed over substantial areas of land and is correspondingly unreliable. The accurate reading of the null rests on the helmsman's skill in keeping the yacht steady and upright, while a 180° ambiguity is occasionally revealed when, for example, you are not certain as to which side of a lightvessel you are and the set has no sense aerial. If this has shaken your faith in radio direction finding, so much the better, for these sets are only *aids* to navigation and undue reliance on them can be dangerous. Let me end with the five questions you must always ask yourself before recording a fix from radio bearings.

Five checks for a radio fix:

1. Do you have recent and reliable information about (a) quadrantal error, or (b) deviation for the instrument?
2. Have you switched off all other electrical apparatus and disconnected all the aerials except the one you will be using?
3. Are you within 25 miles of the beacons chosen for fixing?
4. Are any of them at a narrow angle to the coast or transmitting over land?
5. Do your selected beacons have a wide angle of 'cut'?

Questions

Using either *Reed's Nautical Almanac*, or Vol. 2 of the *Admiralty List of Radio Signals*, find the radio frequencies and call letters of the following beacons:

(a) North Foreland Lt.
(b) Dungeness.
(c) St Catherine's Point.
(d) Berry Head.

(Answers on page 119.)

Chapter Seven

Plotting

Careful plotting makes for shorter voyages and gives reasonable certainty of position at all times, and even though you may be coasting along in plain sight of the shore it is commonsense to work out and follow the most direct route and to check progress made. Look ahead to figures 45 and 46. It is 15 miles by land from Southtown to Marineville and 18 by sea following the shortest route. A yacht leaving Southtown and making for Marineville by merely keeping the shore a mile to starboard all the way will not only have to make a detour to get round the dangerous rocks lying south-west of West Head, and spent an uncomfortable hour in the race off the headland, it will also travel across 25 per cent more sea than a sister ship taking the shortest route. Your job is to find the safest and least time-consuming way of making the voyage, to provide courses for the helmsman to steer, to record progress made and to forecast a time of arrival.

Plotting symbols

Some of these you will know already, but this is the time to complete the list and test your memory. The symbol for a dead reckoning position is a cross and a four-figure time (+ 1725), although occasionally you may see a simple bar across a course line used to denote dead, or deduced, reckoning. DR positions are forecasts based solely on course steered and speed through the water. The estimated position (EP) is your best estimate of position taking into account tide and leeway (and any other factors that may be relevant) and is plotted as a dot within a triangle with the time entered alongside it. The important difference is that EPS are strong and the DRS are weak indications of position. Now answer the following:

1. How would you indicate a fix on the chart?
2. What does a line with two arrowheads on each end mean?
3. When drawing a tidal triangle how do you show the effect of tidal stream?

(Answers on page 119.)

Plotting sheet

You will see many experienced navigators who should know better jotting down data on old envelopes or the margins of charts, but such slapdash ways lead only to red-faced muttered apologies when the sums come out wrong, and it is as well to keep a proper record of work done on a plotting sheet. You will find that the logbooks on sale tend to be more in the nature of diaries for recording past events than suitable vehicles for grouping and employing up-to-date information, and that it is necessary to make up your own plotting sheets.

Figure 47 depicts a comprehensive type of plotting sheet with very full information entered on it for instructional purposes, but the sort that you make for your own use can be much simpler and contain only six columns covering time, log reading, speed, true course, compass course and remarks.

Track

The track is the way you want to go in terms of course and speed over the ground,* and in the planning stage is best referred to as Required Track or the course line. In figures 45 and 46 it is apparent that the dangers off West Head should be given a wide berth, and a perusal of the chart and *Sailing Directions* tells you that there is a shoal patch running south-westward for almost 2 miles from the headland, that overfalls dangerous to small craft can be expected up to $2\frac{1}{2}$ miles off it and that Goat Island has extensive underwater ledges off its north-eastern and south-western extremities. The *Cruising Association Handbook* recommends a 3-mile offing, and your first task is to draw a circle with a 3-mile radius from West

---

* Strictly speaking, the track is the yacht's progress or intended progress across the seabed, but as this is clearly impossible it becomes progress over the chart.

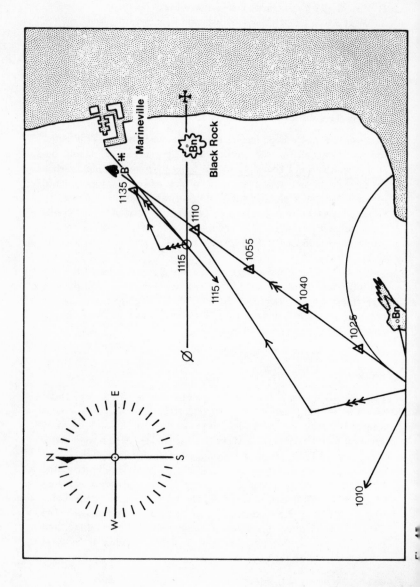

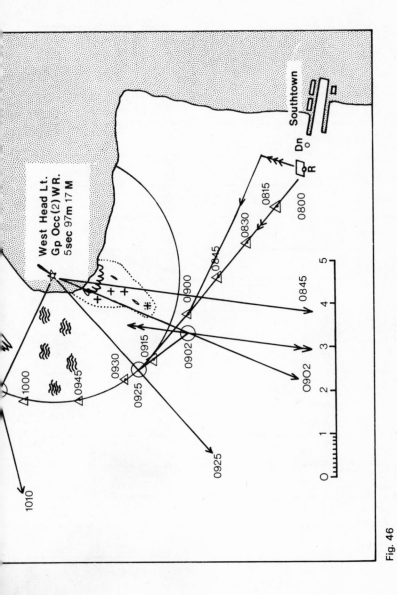

West Head Lt.
Gp Occ(2)W.R.
5sec 97m 17 M

Southtown

Dn

R

0800
0815
0830
0845
0900
0902
0915
0925
0930
0945
1000
1010

Fig. 46

PLOTTING SHEET

TIME	LOG	TRACK	TIDE	RATE	SPEED	WIND	FORCE	L'WAY	CO(T)	VAR	CO(M)	DEV	CO(c)	S.M.G	REMARKS
0800	1120	310°	020°	1·0	4·1		3	NIL	295°	10°W	305°	1°E	304°	4·4	Sea slight Bar. 1023
0845	1123½				4·0				010°	10°W	020°	NIL	020°		West Head Lt.020°(c)
0902	1124½	325°	favourable		4·0	SE	3		023°	10°W	033°	NIL	033		West Head Lt.033°(c)
0925								NIL	325°	10°W	335°	2°W	337°		West Head Lt.060°(c) 3 miles
									050°	10°W	060°	NIL	060°		
													steered as directed		
1010	1130	035°	348°	2·5	5·0	SE	4		118°	10°W	128°	NIL	128°		West Head Lt.128°(c) Goat I. bn 089°(c)
									079°	10°W	089°	NIL	089°	5·1	
								5°P	062°	10°W	072	3°E	069°		
1115	1136					SE	4		050°	10°W	060°	NIL	060°	6·4	LHE Marineville Pier 060°(c) Ø Black Rock and Church 090° (T)
									090°						
1145	1139	045°	345°	1·8	5·0			8°P	074°	10°W	084°	2°E	082°	5·4	ETA Marineville 1145

Distance run – 19 miles by log   Time – 3¾ hours. Average speed over ground – 5·1 knots

Fig. 47

Head and put in course lines running from the departure point – the red buoy off Southtown – and the point of landfall – the black buoy off Marineville – tangential to this circle. In figure 46 the track to be followed during the first part of the voyage is represented by the line from the red buoy in a north-westerly direction and marked with two arrows.

Tidal triangle

At 0800 on a fair summer morning the yacht *Hopeful* has motored out of Southtown harbour, hoisted sail, and is at her departure point near the red buoy. The navigator starts the log and begins to plot and record. He notes the log reading, wind strength and direction and barometic pressure on the plotting sheet and then looks up the tide in the tidal atlas. For the next hour the tide runs 020° at a 1 knot; there is no leeway and the log shows that the fair wind is pushing the yacht along at 4·1 knots. The navigator turns to the chart, marks off 1 sea mile in an 020° direction from the departure point near the red buoy, sets his dividers to 4·1 miles on the latitude scale, puts one point at the end of the tidal stream vector and cuts the track to get his EP for 0900. He draws in the 'course to steer' part of the triangle, carries it across to the compass rose and gets a true figure of 295°. He enters the variation and deviation from the table on the plotting sheet, does the addition and subtraction required and gets 304° as the compass course to steer.

This information is passed to the helmsman, and the navigator finishes the sequence of work by measuring the speed likely to be made good along the track line, noting it on the sheet and dividing it into four to get EPS for every 15 minutes so that if the visibility deteriorated he would have some precise idea of his position. There are no dangers on this course, and no immediate opportunities of obtaining a fix.

Running fix

At 0845 a dank sea-mist has settled over the water, and the only object in sight is West Head lighthouse which by his deviation-free hand-bearing compass bears 020°. The navigator enters it in his 'remarks' column, converts the bearing to a true reading using the course columns for the purpose, plots the line of bearing with the time and notes the log reading in column 2. According to the tidal atlas, the stream is negligible close inshore at this time of day and he watches the log carefully until at 0902 it reads $1124\frac{1}{2}$, signifying that the yacht has run 1 mile since 0845. The second bearing of West Head lighthouse turns out to be 033° by compass. He converts it to true, plots it, carries forward the 0845 position line 1 mile in the direction of the track, plots the transferred position line and examines the fix for validity. It shows the yacht to seaward of her track – a fault on the right side – and a little ahead of where she should be. It seems likely that a small amount of tidal stream is running out of the bay because of a semi-rotary tendency, and although the angle of 'cut' is narrow he feels satisfied that the yacht is clear of the rocky patch south-west of West Head on her present course. He circles the fix, giving it the time of taking the second bearing.

Position by bearing and vertical sextant angle

West Head lighthouse and the shoreline in its vicinity are still the only points of reference in sight, and as there is no sign of a clearance he decides to work out a compass course to bring the yacht onto the 3-mile danger circle and then round the promontory and its offlying dangers by use of a vertical sextant angle. A new track is drawn in tangential to the danger circle; he finds the true course to steer from the compass rose, converts it, and passes the helmsman his new compass course to steer of 337°. There is no tidal information worth acting on, although what stream there is appears to be favourable, and he notes the fact on the plotting sheet. The almanac tells him that the lantern of West Head lighthouse is 97 metres above Mean Higher High Water and that to get a 3-mile offing the vertical sextant angle should be 1°00′. He begins taking the angle between the lighthouse lantern and the breaking sea on the rocks below, and for some time it is less than 1°00′ as the yacht closes the danger circle. At 0925 the sextant gives the desired angle, and a compass bearing taken immediately afterwards provides a fix, as in figure 46. For the next 45 minutes the navigator continues taking the angle at regular intervals, directing the helmsman to steer to starboard when the angle falls below 1°00′ and to port when it reaches that figure.

Cross-bearing fix

At 1010 when the log reads 1130 the navigator takes the compass bearings of West Head lighthouse and the beacon on Goat Island, converts them to true and plots them. He is on track and the fix is circled and timed. What of the tide? The atlas indicates that for the next hour the stream is predicted as running 348° at 2½ knots, and he begins to plot the large tidal triangle in figure 45 on a 1-hour basis, starting with the tidal component. The wind is a little stronger, and as both wind and tide are offshore on this leg of the voyage an allowance must be made for leeway.

Leeway

He stands aft looking at the wake and estimates that the angle between it and a prolongation of the fore-and-aft line is 5°, with the wind pressing on the starboard side making the leeway 5° to port. Entered on the plotting sheet, the figure is added mentally to the original true course to steer obtained from the tidal triangle to give an amended true course of 062°. This figure is converted to a compass course to steer of 069° and passed to the helmsman. The speed made good with a quartering tide and beam wind is measured as 6·4 knots, and the EPS are plotted down the track line at 15-minute intervals. The navigator steps off the remaining distance and notes his ETA (estimated time of arrival) at Marineville as 1145.

Fix by transit and bearing

At 1110 he sees that he will shortly be crossing a line of transit provided by Black Rock beacon and the church on shore, while the pier at Marineville is also visible. At the moment of transitting, he gets the bearing of the left-hand edge of the pier, converts the latter to a true bearing (the line of transit needs no such conversion), and plots a fix at 1115 – see figure 45. He is to seaward of his track and the buoy is in sight: should he direct the helmsman to steer straight for that buoy?

The non-plot result

Figure 48 illustrates what happens if the navigator tells the helmsman to steer for the buoy. The tidal stream is running 345° at a reduced

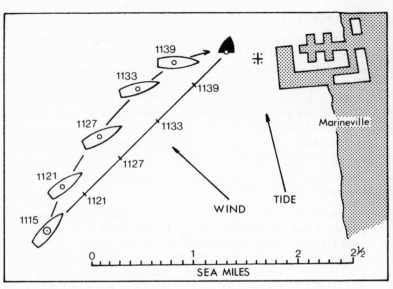

Fig. 48

rate of 1·8 knots by this time, and the 1115 fix shows that he should have allowed 8° of leeway rather than 5°. The helmsman starts off steering north-east but is pushed to port all the time and ends up steering east. The yacht sails a cable more than she should, and this leg of the voyage takes five minutes longer. 'Steering for the buoy' can only be justified when very short distances are involved, and the correct procedure as followed in our example is to construct a tidal triangle for 20 minutes using a third of the predicted tide and a third of the anticipated speed. In figure 45 this resulted in a course to steer 082° and arrival at the landfall buoy 10 minutes before the ETA at Marineville. Figure 47 has the navigator's summary at the foot of the sheet, and he will use this data when making his formal entry in the yacht's log.

Dead reckoning plotting and anticipation of weather changes

Dead reckoning positions were omitted from figures 45 and 46 in the interests of clarity, but you would normally plot them along a track to get a tentative ETA and to check progress. Sailing vessels can

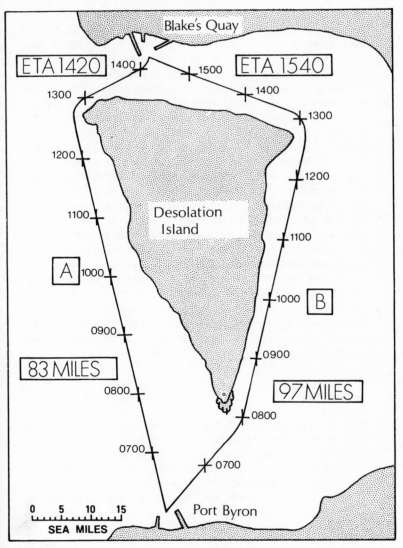

Fig. 49

rarely maintain a constant speed through the water, but motor yachts are able to do so, and figure 49 has been drawn to indicate how a DR plot will help you decide between alternative courses. In the example a 10-knot vessel is due to leave Port Byron at dawn for Blake's Quay, and the navigator has plotted the two ways of getting there. Route 'A' is shorter, but more exposed; route 'B' is longer but traverses sheltered water. The time difference is about an hour and a half, and in calm weather route 'A' is the obvious choice.

However, let us imagine that just before the departure the weather forecast is '... winds light and variable at first, becoming north-westerly Force 6 to 7 soon and veering northerly, gale Force 8 later ...' The terms 'soon' and 'later' have precise meanings, with 'soon' meaning 6–12 hours from the time of issue of the forecast, and 'later' more than 12 hours from the time of issue, and if the forecast is timed for 0530 the strong north-westerly wind can be expected at any time after 1130. Look at route 'A' again. At about 1130 the yacht will be approaching the north-western tip of Desolation Island and a north-westerly wind in such an exposed spot will not only slow you down considerably but may build up punishing waves quite quickly. On route 'B', on the other hand, 1130 finds the yacht tucked under the bulk of Desolation Island and well sheltered from wind and sea. Moreover, even after rounding the north-eastern cape the land to the northward will provide some protection. Dead reckoning, and the forecast, will have confirmed your decision to go the longer, slower, but safer way.

Cone plotting

Adverse winds demand a special type of plotting in so far as sailing craft are concerned, and the basis of cone plotting is that there is less chance of error when going to windward if your tacks are made by reference to time or distance covered. Figure 50 illustrates the point. A sailing yacht is down wind from its home port and can make 60° to the true wind when close-hauled. You start by drawing in a central dotted line on the chart from the destination to your present position and add the 'cone' in the form of two solid lines at 20° from the common origin. At your present position start the first tack at 60° to the dotted line and then zigzag between the extremities, putting in the remaining tacks at 60° to the dotted line. Using the dividers and the

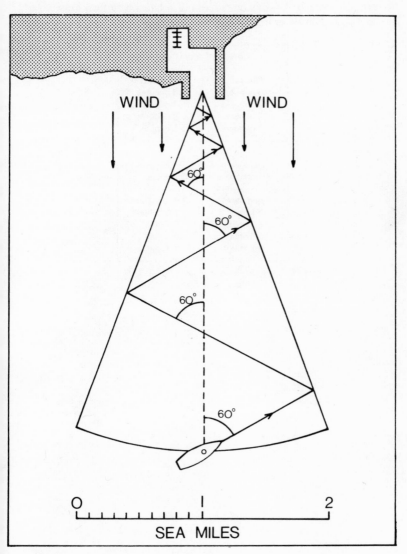

WIND   WIND

60°

60°

60°

60°

O   I   2
SEA MILES

Fig. 50

latitude scale, and assuming a speed of 6 knots, you then draw up a
table based on either time or distance, as follows:

Change of tack (Time)	
Port tack	Starboard tack
10 minutes	16 minutes
12 minutes	7 minutes
5 minutes	3 minutes
2 minutes	1 minute

Change of tack (Distance)	
Port tack	Starboard tack
1 mile	1·6 miles
1·2 miles	0·7 mile
0·5 mile	0·3 mile
0·2 mile	0·1 mile

Chapter Eight

The navigator at work

At this final stage we can put it all together and run through a short voyage with you as the navigator and me, the author, butting in occasionally with queries and reminders.

Figure 51 is the backdrop to the story, with the good ship *Hopeful* lying peacefully at anchor in North River just before dawn. Last night, the skipper had hinted that he would like to sail round to South Dock on the following day, and it begins when your alarm goes off with a heart-stopping jangle at 0630. You roll over, unzip your sleeping bag sufficiently to switch on the radio, and retreat into the warmth once more. The shipping forecast is on Radio Two (1500 m or 200 kHz) at 0633, and the general synopsis speaks of a pattern of westerly winds over the British Isles, gales in Denmark Strait and south-east Iceland but no strong winds in the southern North Sea. North River is in the Thames sea area for forecast purposes, and as the detailed forecast emerges you make a note of the relevant bits for the log. Humber, Thames and Dover are dealt with together, with westerly winds Force 3 or 4 expected and occasional light rain and poor visibility. Reports from coastal stations at Gorleston (to the north of your position) and Manston (to the south) speak of an over-cast sky, visibility down to a mile and a half and the current as westerly Force 3. It is raining at Portland (to the westward), where sea-mist has reduced visibility to 1,000 yards.

To sail, or not to sail?

You consider all the known facts and look at the large-scale chart (figure 51). A west wind is a fair one out of North River, will be just forward of the beam on the long leg down the coast and on the nose for the last part of the trip. The sea is likely to be smooth – being in

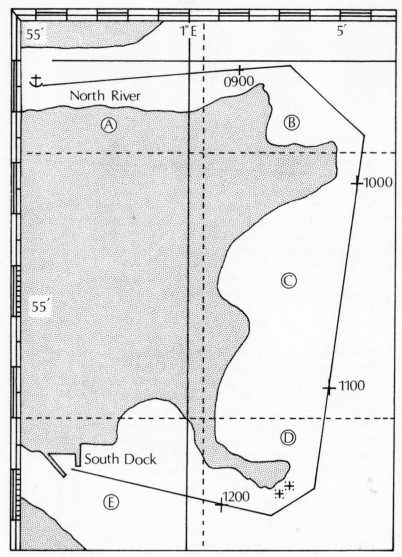

Fig. 51

the lee of the land – but the visibility is poor and may deteriorate. You slide back the hatch and patter forward to take down the riding light. It is a cool, grey day but there is no weight in the wind or sign of an angry sky to windward. The morning air smells good, and you come to a decision. As far as the navigational department is concerned, *Hopeful* can sail.

When to leave?

Tide is a major factor in deciding when to leave, and you leaf through *Reed's Nautical Almanac* to get the time of local high water. It is not due until the afternoon, and a little mental calculation tells you that low water is at 0700. *Reed's* also indicates that it is two days before springs, and as the tidal streams will be strong it is all the more imperative to use them to the full. The tidal atlas shows the flood running in from the north-east just after 0700 so that the yacht will have a foul tide leaving the river, a fair one down the coast and a neutral or negligible amount of tide on the approach to South Dock, where high water is at 1303. Now to plot the DR assuming an average speed of 4 knots and an 0800 departure. Look at figure 51 and answer the following questions:

1. How far is it from your present position to South Dock?
2. At 4 knots, what will be the ETA?
(Answers on page 119.)

Sailing Directions indicate that the lock gates are open from an hour before to an hour after high water, from 1203 to 1403, and an 0800 departure and 1245 ETA seem to give a reasonable margin. You are now in a position to see the skipper and give the information he will require. You tell him that the trip is feasible, and that 0800 is a sensible time for departure. The ETA is 1245, and the voyage will be in three parts. On leaving North River you will have a fair wind and a foul tide. On the coastal leg the wind will be abeam and the tide fair, and on the approach to South Dock, the wind will be ahead and the tide negligible.

Checking instruments and charts

Breakfast is being prepared in the galley, and as the yacht swings to breast the flood stream you decide to check the deviation of both compasses on an easterly heading. As dawn breaks you unlash the tiller and give *Hopeful* a sheer to starboard so that she faces the rising sun momentarily as you note the reading first on one compass and then the other. Satisfied that there has been no change for either compass on an easterly heading you put the hand-bearer away and get out the charts you will need, ranging them in order of use. Sharpened pencils, a parallel ruler, dividers, compasses and a soft rubber are in their tray at the side of the chart table, and *Sailing Directions*, *Reed's Nautical Almanac* and the tidal atlas are ready on the shelf behind. You check that the echosounder is working, put the DF set on the right wavelength for the local group of beacons and make the background entries in the log and on the plotting sheet. Over breakfast you advise the skipper of the finer points in the weather forecast and agree that full main and number two genoa seem to be the right combination for the forecasted conditions. After breakfast – having helped with the washing-up – you settle down to work out the first course to steer as the crew haul short on the chain preparatory to getting the anchor inboard. (Now look at figure 52 as the plotting begins.)

Two tidal triangles and a fix

Sailing Directions and the tidal atlas have yielded the information that the early flood stream in the mouth of North River runs at up to 2 knots at springs and sets south south-westward. By interpolating between the direction given in the Pilot, the almanac and the atlas you come up with 197° at 2 knots. You decide to begin on a ½-hour basis, and as from the first tidal triangle in figure 52 and a comparison of the 0830 DR and EP it is clear that *Hopeful* will be falling behind from the start, an early fix to check progress is desirable. The compass course to steer is 040°, and this is passed to the helmsman as the anchor comes over the gunwale and the yacht begins to move purposefully through the water. At 0825 the visibility is down to a mile, but you can still see both banks; a beacon to the north-west and a flagstaff on the southern shore offer a good 'cut' of about 90° and are used to get a fix. The 0830 fix by cross-bearings shows you to be north of your track and ahead of EP, indicating that you have probably over-estimated the strength of the tidal stream. Now for a question. What is the speed made good between 0800 and 0830? (*Answer on page 119.*)

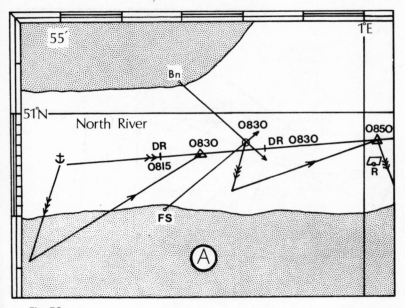

Fig. 52

Time to try another combination of figures which recognise that the tide has less push than anticipated while the wind is giving a better speed than was hoped for. Working from the 0830 fix, you plot for twenty minutes on the amended data of a tidal stream setting 197° at 1½ knots and a speed through the water of 4½ knots. The resultant EP is 2½ cables north of the red buoy, and when passing the compass course to steer to the helmsman you add that he can expect to see a red buoy to starboard in a few minutes' time.

Fix by transit and bearing and running fix

The red buoy comes abeam at 0850 and, being back on track, you look for a new basis for calculation, settling on half an hour. The tidal atlas shows a fork of the stream at this point, and your best estimate is that at just before 0900 it runs 158° at 1½ knots. Laying off ¾ mile in a 158° direction, you complete the triangle and come up with 069° as the course to steer. The visibility is still poor and the

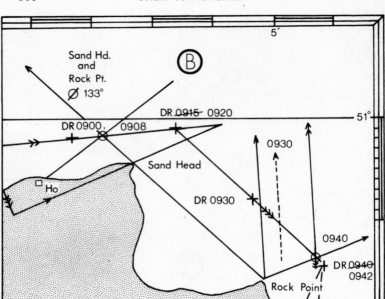

Fig. 53

wind is dropping, but at 0908 (see figure 53) you glimpse Rock Point emerging clear of Sand Head on a transit of 133° and cross it with the bearing of a house on the nearer shore. You are still on track, but behind on DR. Now for some questions.

1. How far ahead is the 0915 DR position?
2. If present speed over the ground is $3\frac{3}{4}$ knots when will you get there?

(*Answers on page 119.*)

At 0910 a rain squall, the first of the day, sweeps in from the west blotting out the land altogether and you decide to change course 'blind' when the log or clock shows that the old 0915 DR position has been reached. (Note that in figure 53 the old time has not been rubbed out after being found wanting: it is neatly deleted and a new time inserted alongside.)

The next true course is 134° but as the tidal atlas shows the stream setting 140° at 1½ knots east of Sand Head you consider a tidal triangle can hardly be meaningful and convert the true course to compass course, treating the tide as additional speed. The wind has picked up again to give 4¼ knots, and you add the speed and tide together to get 5¾ knots, finding from the new DR that you should only be two minutes behind when off Rock Point. The euphoria that this discovery confers soon evaporates as the wind falls away again and you are down to three knots. At 0930 Rock Point comes mistily into view, and you take its bearing, convert it and plot it. Ten minutes later you get a second bearing of the point and give it similar treatment. Now for the calculations. In ten minutes a 1½-knot tide will have pushed *Hopeful* 2½ cables down her track, and in the same time she will have covered a ½ mile at her present speed. (The dotted line in figure 53 is to show that the left portion between the 0930 position line and the transferred position line is the tidal component and the right portion ascribable to the yacht's passage through the water.) The transfer of the 0930 position line ¾ of a mile down the track gives the 0940 fix.

A wreck problem, and a fix by sounding and radiobeacon

The next tidal triangle is of the orthodox 1-hour type – the stream setting 198° at 1 knot (information from the tidal diamond in figure 54), and the speed 3 knots. Ten minutes after receiving the compass course the helmsman puts his head down the companionway and asks, 'I can see a green buoy ahead: which side shall I leave it?' What will you tell him? (*Answer on page 119.*)

The land falls away as you cross Bride's Bay and at 1038 you switch on the echosounder to obtain a position line from the steep northern edge of The Ridge. At 1040 the expected sudden change from a corrected depth of 25 metres to one of under 10 metres takes place, and almost simultaneously you get a good null from a radiobeacon 12 miles away and are able to plot a true bearing of 330°. The fix shows *Hopeful* to seaward of her track and although you decide to plot the fix you have one principal reservation about its accuracy. What do you think it is? (*Answer on page 119.*) Your copy of *East Coast Rivers* suggests that after half-flood the stream on the outer part of The Ridge is deflected seawards, and this is confirmed by the tidal atlas so that you estimate the tidal set at 115° and the rate as 0·6 of a knot. Plotting for 40 minutes, you draw in a new track and course

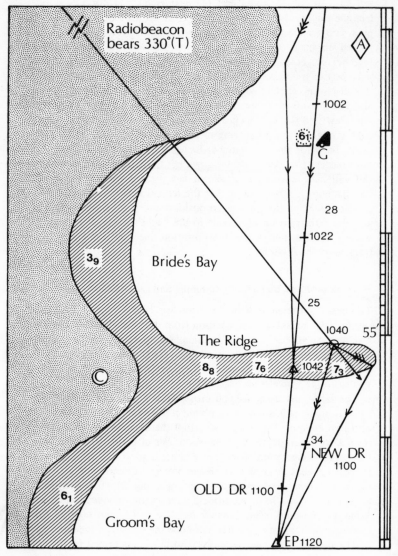

Radiobeacon
bears 330°(T)

1002

6₁
G

28

1022

Bride's Bay

3₉

25

1040   55'

The Ridge

8₈   7₆   1042   7₃

34
NEW DR
1100

OLD DR 1100

6₁

Groom's Bay

EP 1120

A

Fig. 54

to steer, passing a compass course of 200° to the helmsman in due course. *Hopeful* is slowing down because the failing wind is only giving a speed of 3 knots and the flood tide is slackening. At this point the skipper asks you how far the yacht is behind her dead reckoning. Is your answer (a) 8 minutes, (b) 12 minutes, (c) 16 minutes, or (d) 20 minutes? (*Answer on page 119.*)

Two fixes and the Twelfth's Rule

At 1120 Cape Sandra lighthouse comes in view bearing 42° on the starboard bow, and at 1132 it bears 84°. The tide is negligible, a constant course is maintained between the times when the bearings were taken and the log shows two-thirds of a mile covered in 12 minutes. The 1132 fix is plotted as in figure 55; you are still to seaward of the track, and this time believe that it is because you have not allowed for leeway.

After giving the new course, you look at the chart and realise that Cape Sandra Shoal lies ahead with very little water on it at low tide,

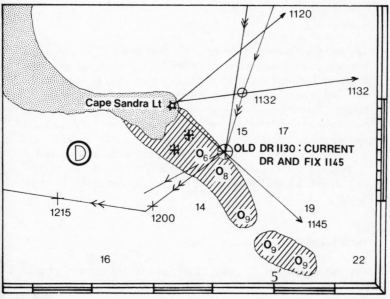

Fig. 55

and although it is now getting on for high water it seems prudent to check the probable depth before crossing. The tables indicated that the rise of tide today is 4·2 metres, and each twelfth will therefore be 0·35 of a metre. Low water was at 0700, and at 1100, four hours later, the height is going to be one-twelfth, plus two-twelfths, plus three twelfths, plus three twelfths – making nine-twelfths in all. Nine times 0·35 is 3·15 and adding 0·7 for the sounding gives 3·85 metres as the depth of water at 1100 and something over 4 metres at 1130. *Hopeful* draws less than 2 metres, and can safely cross the shoal. The new DR shows you are 15 minutes behind schedule, and a fix at 1145 confirms it. (A slightly different technique: echosounder on the edge of the shoal and the bearing of the lighthouse.) The wind is drawing ahead, and on the next leg you decide to allow 10° for leeway. In figure 55 immediately south of the lighthouse the course line with the single arrow shows the allowance for leeway. The true course is 234°, there is no tide to speak of, and you make it 244° − 10° of port leeway – before applying deviation and variation and getting the compass course to steer.

Anticipation

The yacht is close-hauled and moving towards the 1200 DR position preparatory to changing course for South Dock when you review the situation. The wind is ahead, the tide is neither a help nor a hindrance (although it will be ebbing against you after 1300), and you are 15 minutes behind DR. You sketch out a 'cone' plot for working to windward up to South Dock and find that with a speed of three knots and an ability to sail 60° to the true wind your ETA is 1430 – too late to lock in for the night. The straight line distance is over 4 miles, but the tacking distance is nearly 8. You approach the skipper and suggest 5 knots under engine to reach the destination in ample time.

Three-bearing fix and harbour signals

The tide is full and the wind ahead, so that for the first part of the run up to South Dock there is little more to do than to convert the true course (which is also the track) to a compass course to steer.

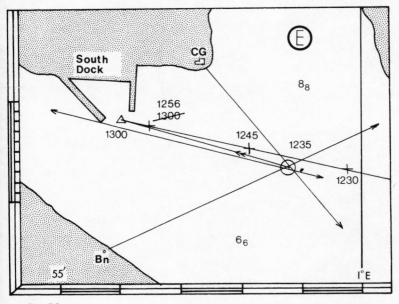

Fig. 56

The visibility improves, and at 1235 (figure 56) you are able to take
a set of three bearings of the Coastguard hut, the left-hand edge of the
pier and a beacon on the south shore. A minor correction to the
compass course follows, and such good progress is made under
engine in smooth water that your last DR ahead claws back 4 minutes of
lost time. Your original ETA is eleven minutes out, but you feel a certain
satisfaction at having made a creditable passage in such fluky weather.

One final duty remains. You consult *Sailing Directions* and the
Cruising Association Handbook so as to give the skipper his briefing
on a strange port. You tell him that the lock gates are at the root of
the eastern pier and that signals relating to vessels using it are dis-
played from a gantry on the port side. Three vertical red balls mean
no entry, two white ones signify that vessels can enter and one black
one that they can leave. You remind him that it is early closing day
and that if stores are required they will have to wait until next morning. You clean off the charts, turn off the instruments, put away the
books and go on deck to give a hand with the fenders. You have
done your work for today, and done it well.

Answers

	Buoy 'A'	Buoy 'B'
Shape	can	spherical
Topmark	two cones, point to point, (hourglass)	sphere
System	cardinal	lateral
Colour of buoy	black over white	red and white horizontal bands
Function	a westerly cardinal mark	a middle ground buoy
Meaning	pass to the westward	pass either side

(d) weed

p. 37   1.   050° (T)

      2.   the vessel would run aground

Chapter Three

p. 43   4·5 metres or 14 feet, 9 inches (By using the Twelfths Rule, as described on page 43, the height of tide is $3\frac{1}{4}$ metres + chart datum depth at $1\frac{1}{4}$ metres, making $4\frac{1}{2}$ metres in all)

p. 45   1.   0·7 metres or 2 feet, 4 inches, *plus* the charted sounding of 4 feet, making the depth 6 feet, 4 inches or 1·9 metres

      2.   0420

      3.   0535

p. 52   1.   yes

      2.   2 knots

      3.   060°

Chapter Four

p. 59   1.   335° (T)

      2.   243° (T)

      3.   020° (T)

p. 60   1.   180° (C)

      2.   250° (C)

      3.   190° (C)

p. 66   177° (T)

Chapter Five

p. 72   1.   the two black conical buoys

      2.   no

      3.   (a)   51° 44·1′ N, 5° 18·6′ W

          (b)   51° 43·5′ N, 5° 18·6′ W

          (c)   51° 43′ 33″ N, 5° 21′ 29″ W

          (d)   51° 42′ 21″ N, 5° 18′ 46″ W

p. 79   1.   190°

      2.   a piece of leather with a hole in it

      3.   two strips of leather

      4.   (a)   51° 41′ N

          (b)   51° 41′ 57″ N

          (c)   51° 43′ 51″ N

Chapter Six

p. 82 The effect of tidal stream

p. 91 (a) 301·1 kHz NF

     (b) 310·3 kHz DU

     (c) 291·9 kHz CP

     (d) 318   kHz BHD

Chapter Seven

p. 93 1. a circle around a dot, or a circle at the intersection of two or more position lines

     2. a transferred position line

     3. with three arrowheads

Chapter Eight

p. 107 1. 19 sea miles

     2. 1245 hours

p. 108 3·7 knots

p. 110 1. three-quarters of a mile

     2. in 12 minutes, at 0920 hours

p. 111 (a) Either side. The vessel is travelling with the flood stream, and in a deep-draught ship you would leave the buoy to starboard. However, this submerged danger has been swept by wire drag to a cleared depth of 6·1 metres and presents no threat to a yacht drawing less than 2 metres of water

     (b) the signal has passed over land and may be unreliable

p. 113 12 minutes

Bibliography

A. Coles, *North Brittany Pilot*, Adlard Coles Limited, London, 1976.

Cruising Association, *Cruising Association Handbook*, London, 1971.

E. Delmar-Morgan, *North Sea Harbours and Pilotage*, Adlard Coles Limited, London, 1976.

ESL Bristol, *An Introduction to Coastal Navigation*, Bristol, 1973.

ESL Bristol, *A Seaman's Guide to Basic Chartwork*, Bristol, 1970.

Hydrographer of the Navy, *Chart 5011* (book edition), Taunton, 1973.

Hydrographer of the Navy, *Admiralty List of Lights and Fog Signals*, Volume A, Taunton, 1974.

Hydrographer of the Navy, *Admiralty List of Radio Signals*, Volume 2, Taunton, 1974.

Hydrographer of the Navy, *The Mariner's Handbook*, Taunton, 1973.

Hydrographer of the Navy, Tidal Stream Atlas *The English and Bristol Channels*, Taunton, 1973.

Hydrographer of the Navy, *West Coasts of England and Wales Pilot*, Taunton, 1974.

D. A. Moore, *Basic Principles of Marine Navigation*, Kandy Publications, Sevenoaks, 1973.

O. M. Watts (ed.), *Reed's Nautical Almanac*, Sunderland, 1976.

T. J. Williams, *Coastal Navigation*, Thomas Reed, Sunderland, 1974.

C. Worth, *Yacht Navigation and Voyaging*, London, 1935.

Index